Eighteenth Century French Novelists

and the Novel

Eighteenth Century French Novelists

and the Novel

by

Lawrence W. Lynch

French Literature Publications Company
York, South Carolina
1979

PREFACE

A study on the eighteenth-century French novel would be incomplete without some sort of preface; they were an indispensable part of the main work. Caution must be exercised, however, because those old preambles often contained promises which were not meant to be kept.

In writing this work on the eighteenth-century French novel, I have only one main goal: to call due attention to the theoretical writings of the major French novelists of the eighteenth century. These texts have been too frequently overlooked in favor of secondary and often unrelated criticism. And I am convinced that the actual authors were in a better position to evelute their works than anyone else.

Among the "major" authors selected for examination here, some omissions will be apparent. These are due mainly to the lack of availability of theoretical treatment of the genre by the novelists. I did not treat Lesage due to a lack of critical material, The same is true for Restif de la Bretonne. Bernardin de Saint-Pierre was omitted because his approach to the novel parallels that of Jean-Jacques Rousseau. The most obvious omission is Voltaire; yet I assume that his particular style and methods are so unique that he can be easily separated from the general confines of this study.

In further pursuit of the goal announced, I felt it appropriate to translate the French texts in question, so as to make them available to as large an audience of readers as possible. When required to decide between the preservation of the author's original style or its modernization, I invariably chose the latter. I bear full responsibility for the translations in the chapters which follow, with the exception of Sade's "Reflections on the Novel"; this particular document was recently published in English by the Grove Press, and is reproduced here with permission. Portions of this work have appeared in article form in the following reviews, and are reproduced with permission. I wish to thank the editor of *French Review* for his permission to use my "The Critical Preface to *Les Egarements du coeur et de l'esprit*" (Vol. 51, no. 5), and the editor of *Kentucky Romance Quarterly* for use of my "Laclos and Fictional Standards" (Vol. 25, no. 2).

Finally, since brevity was a characteristic to be admired in eighteenth-century prefaces, I merely add three expressions of gratitude: to the various members of the University of Iowa faculty who assisted me in the earlier forms of this work, to the Grants and Research Funding Committee and the College of Humanities Faculty Development Committee of Southeast Missouri State University for financial assistance.

CONTENTS

I
INTRODUCTION

The novel was the dominant literary genre in eighteenth-century France. When compared to the production, either in quantity or quality, of drama, the epic, even philosophical literature, not to mention verse, the supremacy of prose fiction is unquestionable. Evidence of this dominance comes from many sources: Gustave Lanson stated that the novel was the only artistic genre in progress in the eighteenth century.[1] More recently, Roger Laufer, who compared the style of eighteenth-century French prose fiction to the *rococo* movement in the plastic arts, and who considered the *rococo* as the only discernable style between the classical and the romantic eras, also compared the place of the eighteenth-century novel with that of the contemporary film in the hierarchy of the arts.[2] Daniel Mornet accounted for the novel's success with some interesting insights: according to his *La Pensée française au XVIIIe siècle,* since there were no antecedents for the novel among the ancients and the classical authors, the novel was considered as a frivolous and morally corrupt genre.[3] And since the novel was nothing but a form of entertainment, it enjoyed total freedom from classical restraints; such were the reasons for its survival.

The fact that the novel was technically not a great genre may have indeed been the means for its development. Efforts by Voltaire and others to preserve the classical concept of tragedy were to no avail. The most revered of genres, the epic, had weakened to the point of being transformed into parody, Boileau's *Le Lutrin* and Pope's *Dunciad* providing some notable examples. In poetry, André Chénier was the primary representative, although his reputation dates from late in the eighteenth century. Poetry as such was rather neglected throughout the Enlightenment.

In addition to being the dominant literary genre, the novel

was also the most poorly defined genre. There had been a *roman* in the seventeenth century, but it was characterized by dislocated, insipid and adventurous plots such as are found in the works of La Calprenède, D'Urfé, Scarron, and Furetière. There were, of course, exceptions; *La Princesse de Clèves* is the most prominent one.

Among critics, the concept of novel amounted to disdain; it suffices to quote some of the more distinguished judgments. In Boileau's *Art poétique,* the novel did in fact occupy a place in the hierarchy of genres, but a rather ignominious one:

> In a frivolous novel all is easily excused;
> It suffices that fiction should rapidly amuse;
> Excessive rigor would then be out of place.[4]

Boileau was no more a legislator of the novel than he was of the classical drama; he merely consolidated everything that had been accomplished in practice before him. His opinion of the novel is denunciatory, and had no bearing on the masterpiece novels of the century which followed; yet similar unfavorable opinions persisted for decades after him.

Voltaire, Boileau's successor in terms of respect for classicism, put even more distance between good literature and the bad, i.e., novels: "If some new novels appear even today, and if they amuse our foolish youths for a time, true men of letters scorn them."[5]

Finally, the most enlightened work of the Age of Enlightenment, *L'Encyclopédie,* brought no support to the novel. Le Chevalier de Jaucourt, the author of the article "Roman" in Volume XIV, defined it as a "fictional narration of diverse marvelous or plausible adventures of human life." His definition shows little progress from Boileau's, and the only novels worthy of mention by Jaucourt were those of Fénelon, Hamilton, Fielding, Richardson, and Rousseau. As for the others:

> . . .the majority of other novels which have succeeded
> them in this century, are either productions devoid of
> originality, or which ruin one's taste, or, even worse,
> obscene portraits at which decent people are shocked.

Thus the novel provided a common ground for normally hostile parties such as Jesuits and Jansenists, Voltaire and Rousseau. All agreed that the novel should be condemned for social or artistic reasons.

The focus of this study and of the accompanying texts is the concept of the novel of French authors of the eighteenth century, their attitude toward works of prose fiction, their own and others. These critical texts are largely ignored in studies on the Enlightenment. They reveal, in the first years of the century, a general disdain for the novel; the very authors of novels, Montesquieu, Prévost, and Rousseau, for example, denounced their own genre in terms reminiscent of their critics' remarks:

> Here you see novels, whose authors are a type of poets who shock both the language of the mind and that of the heart.—Montesquieu, *Lettres persanes*, Letter 137.

> These pleasant fancies, engendered by the human mind in one of those outbursts of imagination, force it to depart from the true and the plausible, and are instead concerned with excessively supernatural ideas, which carry it beyond its own limits.—Prévost, *"Réflexions sur les romans,"* in *Le Pour et Contre*.

> Theaters are necessary in large cities, and novels are necessary for corrupt people.—Rousseau, the Author's Preface to *La Nouvelle Héloïse*.

This negative attitude toward the genre reached a climax in 1761 when Diderot rejected the accomplishments of French prose fiction in favor of those of Samuel Richardson:

> Up till now, people have understood by the term *novel* a string of frivolous and imaginary events, the reading of which was dangerous for good taste and morals. I would prefer that another name be found for Richardson's works.[6]

Diderot's search for another term for Richardson's works coincided with the novelists' attempt to avoid the pejorative label of novel. When the actual word *roman* appeared in the works to be discussed, it was far more often than not pejorative. In the first part of the century, it referred to the *romans romanesques* of the preceding era; in the mid-eighteenth century, it was used to condemn those works which we consider to be masterpieces today. An excellent point of reference is the fifth chapter of Georges May's *Le Dilemme du roman au XVIIIe siècle,* where May demonstrates that novelists frequently incorporated the word *histoire* in their titles, and intentionally played on its ambiguous connotations of story and history.[7] No one would really expect to find the word "novel" in the title of a work of fiction; in Prévost's case, however, the term *histoire* appeared with a frequency in his titles that was more than coincidental. Other evasive tactics used by the French novelists were more conventional: they "wrote" journals, memoirs, letters, and auto-biographies—in short—anything but novels. Marivaux's Marianne reminds her reader at the beginning of Part VIII of her auto-biography: "Instead of a true story, you believed that you were reading a novel. You have forgotten that it was my life story which I was relating to you."

The fundamental paradox of the eighteenth-century French novel resides in the fact that everyone hated the novel by defini-tion, yet everyone was satisfied to write and to read them. Not content to condemn the genre that they exercised, the novelists invented devices which would separate themselves even further from their works. Montesquieu, Rousseau, and Laclos purported to be no more than *éditeurs* of the letters they published. Mari-vaux and Prévost relegated their responsibility to discoverers of manuscripts and impersonal witnesses. Few authors dared sign their works, Rousseau being a noteworthy exception. And their titles abounded in ellipses, asterisks, abbreviations, and initials, for example Crébillon's *Lettres de la Marquise de M*** au Comte de R****.

Besides being condemned for esthetic reasons, the novel was denounced on the basis of moral principles, as witnessed in the preceding criticism by Jaucourt, Diderot and Rousseau. The reasons for these condemnations of immorality are vague. On the other hand, eighteenth-century novelists abandoned more and more the archetypes of princes, dukes and lords, in favor of members of the lower classes. Marivaux's Jacob de la Vallée is the best known example. According to May, Marivaux also attracted criticism for the scene of Mme Dutour and the coach-man in Part II of *La Vie de Marianne,* where the street language and verbal exchanges were too graphic to meet with critical approval.[8] There were more specific points for condemnation: Prévost, like Defoe, dared to select a virtuous harlot as his heroine, a choice denounced by Montesquieu, among others. Elsewhere, the novelists, especially Crébillon *fils*, Diderot and Laclos, treated sex and eroticism in their texts, but in an obliquely paraphrased language that is far from being vulgar when judged by modern criteria. Sade is of course in a category by himself.

At one time or another, in any case, the novelists unanimously felt a need to defend their works against reproaches of immorality, and proclaimed the dual Horatian goal of *utile et dulci*. Crébillon *fils* wrote "to censure vices and follies." Prévost labeled *Manon Lescaut* "a moral treatise, pleasantly reduced to practice." Rousseau, unwittingly emphasizing the inherent contradiction between his concept of the novel and his actual practice, introduced *La Nouvelle Héloïse* with the remark that novels were necessary, but necessary for corrupt people. The point made was that letters, memoirs and "authentic" stories could in no way be harmful, since they were "true." Moral respectability was also the goal aimed at by Laclos:

> It appears to me at least that one renders a useful service
> to morality when one reveals the means employed by the
> wicked to corrupt the good, and I am confident that
> these letters can contribute positively to that purpose.
> (*Les Liaisons dangereuses*, "Préface du rédacteur")

In technical terms, the novel was not a great genre because it was a *new* genre; thus there is a need to examine the actual authors' critical texts on their concept of the genre. The novel had indeed been omitted from the classical ordering of genres, as Mornet indicated; new ground was being explored, and there were apparently no rules to be observed. In short, the novelist was at liberty to shape his own artistic form.

The form characterized by the French romances prior to 1700 was obviously inadequate as a means of expression by the authors who followed. The variety of their narrative devices—journals, histories, memoirs and letters—are more than evasive tactics. These devices are also artistic processes, not without their own rules, that were adopted to express the authors' thoughts and sentiments. This fact is too often overlooked by the critics, including the authors as critics. The value of *Le Paysan parvenu* is significantly enhanced by the fact that it is the memoirs of Jacob de la Vallée; the memoir convention permits entry into all levels of society, as do the various insights of the author. *Les Liaisons dangereuses* is not imaginable other than in letter form.

There was no lack of theory for the eighteenth-century French novel; in fact, there was a great wealth of theory. For this reason, the novelists will be examined individually. In the passages discussed, an acute consciousness of writing is manifested, and one of writing novels in particular. Items such as prefaces, *avertissements, avis au lecteur, préfaces de l'éditeur,* etc. deserve special attention, for they were the site of the theoretical battle of the novel. The content of these introductions varies widely: some are mere promises of authenticity or "false fronts." Others are defense mechanisms at most. Still others are essential because they are often the only place where an author discussed his work in serious terms. Montesquieu is a good example. The original preface to *Les Lettres persanes* serves mostly to defend authenticity and to maintain anonymity. The second preface, "Quelques Réflexions sur *les Lettres persanes*," written thirty years later, cast the work in a completely different light, as a novel.

Only the most pertinent texts, those which provide the broadest impression of a particular author's idea of *le roman,* are provided. Other miscellaneous but essential judgments are accounted for in the introductions to each writer.

The introductory materials were also a means of separating a particular work from other works of the same nature. It seems that in eighteenth-century France, it was acceptable to write *novels,* on the condition that they not be presented as *novels.* Individuality is a very human characteristic, but hypocrisy was also involved. Both Crébillon *fils* and Marivaux wrote memoir novels, but they were at odds over its proper form. And Rousseau refuted Diderot's definition of the letter novel in *L'Eloge de Richardson,* while reserving superiority for himself. In reality, he was jealous of Richardson, and vindictive, because Diderot had had nothing to say on Rousseau's *La Nouvelle Héloïse* in *L'Eloge.* In defense of the novelists, the problems of censure and persecution should at least be mentioned. The authorities in the eighteenth century went to great length in suppressing questionable or objectionable passages in new works. When a work was permitted to be published, the approval may have been merely tacit, with the officials turning their eyes away, but all the while reserving the right to outlaw it. These practices may account for the advisability of stating moral purposes, and for some of the inconsistencies in the novelists' theoretical writings.

In spite of the preceding developments, which seem to present an unfavorable portrait of the French novel in terms of theory, there were still optimistic moments. Crébillon *fils* observed in 1738 that the novel could be the most artistic of literary genres, but only if it followed the guidelines of the classical comedy. In 1762, after the great successes of Samuel Richardson's novels, Prévost stated that the novel could accomplish all of the ambitious goals of good literature, particularly moral ones, if it were controlled with the mastery of a Richardson. Near the end of the century, after improvements in France as well as abroad, Laclos was able to treat the novel in completely objective terms. He adeptly pointed to the fundamental paradox of the novel:

> Of all the genres produced by literature, there are few of
> lesser esteem than that of novels; but there is none that is
> more universally sought after or more avidly read.[9]

Laclos went so far as to subordinate the previously venerated genres, history and drama, to the novel. It is only logical that this positive opinion of the novel should appear after the considerable progress made since the first part of the century. Yet such optimism was rare, and achieved only after a long and difficult struggle.

Progress was made nonetheless. Since the very definition of *novel* was under question in the eighteenth century, it is only appropriate that technical, external definitions be examined. In 1694, *Le Dictionnaire de l'Académie* defined *roman* as follows: "Romans: Ouvrages en prose contenant des aventures fabuleuses d'amour et de guerre." (Novels: Prose works containing prodigious adventures of love and of war.) There is nothing wrong with this definition, given its date. In fact, when compared to Boileau's and even Jaucourt's, the definition of *L'Académie française* is quite progressive. In spite of its brevity and a possisible pejorative connotation of the word "fabuleuses," it provides a fairly accurate picture of the novel's *status quo* at the end of the seventeenth century. The 1694 definition still falls short of accounting for the improvement in the genre in the following century. It was only in 1798 that the *Dictionnaire de l'Académie* changed the entry under *roman* for the first time, and with some important modifications; in 1798, it read: "Roman: Ouvrage contenant des fictions qui représentent des aventures rares dans la vie, et le développement entier des passions humaines." (Novel: A Work containing fictions which represent rare adventures in life, and the entire progression of human passions.) Although arbitrary like any other definition, the conceptual progress indicated here is far more in alignment with those works published between 1694 and 1798. The efforts of French writers to present a *tableau de la vie humaine* were successful, at least to the point of convincing the *Académiciens.* The identification of "rare" situations in human life bears more affinity with *Les Egarements du coeur et de l'esprit* and with *Manon Lescaut* than does "Aventures fabuleuses d'amour et de guerre."

This progress was merely a logical result, based on prior accomplishments. Progress was also detected among the eight authors studied, yet it was brief, hesitant, and insufficient, ironically enough, to convince authors such as Diderot, who still chose to denounce the French novel as late as 1761.

The advancement of the concept of *le roman* in eighteenth-century France should have been more substantial before 1798. Based on the texts presented, the favorable opinions found in Laclos and in *Le Dictionnaire de l'Académie* should have been more general and gradual. Unfortunately, such was not the case.

The somewhat "optimistic" moments found in the criticism of the eighteenth-century French novel by Crébillon and Prévost remain as *reservations;* neither is as unqualified or as complete as Laclos' praise of the genre in his review of *Cecilia:*

> Is it not necessary for novels, like any other work, to
> entertain, instruct and be interesting? And since no path
> has been prescribed to arrive at this fundamental goal,
> will it be concluded that it is easier not to deviate? We
> are inclined to believe, however, that few works require

a more profound knowledge of man's heart and mind,
and this knowledge does not seem to us as being easy to
acquire.[10]

The conservatism of Crébillon and Prévost could be excused by
their early date of appearance in the century; Diderot, Rousseau
and Sade were, in contrast, in a position to evaluate objectively
the entire spectrum of Enlightenment prose fiction, and they
failed to do so. Keeping in mind that they had to contend with
the complete production in the genre, and furthermore that the
position of the modern reader concerning art in the novel is even
more privileged, Diderot's and Rousseau's criticism of their
fellow writers still remains problematic.

It must be concluded that improvement in the concept of
the novel came primarily from improvement in practice, not
from theory; the degree of art attained in the actual texts in
1760 was far more advanced than the ideas of *le roman* expressed
at the same date. However, the retrograde concept of *le roman,*
which is evident from my quotations of the novelists, did not
bring about the disappearance of the novel; on the contrary,
the genre evolved into a coherent, unified and realistic narrative
form, also known as *le roman.*

The French novelists' discussion of the novel in the eighteenth century shows that the novel was just as difficult to define then as it is today. It was surely something less than E. M.
Forster's recent definition as ". . .a fiction in prose of a certain
extent."[11] And it was surely something more than an epic in
prose, as earlier critics preferred to believe, and more than "productions devoid of originality," as defined by Jaucourt in
L'Encyclopédie. If the novel is so impossible to define categorically, it can nonetheless be recognized in the Enlightenment
by some common characteristics. Marivaux's *La Vie de Marianne*
demonstrates as well as possible what constituted a novel in the
mid-eighteenth century, obviously before such innovative works
as *Jacques le fataliste* and *Les Liaisons dangereuses* (see my
chapter on Marivaux).

In their search for the "key" to the mystery of the French
novel of the eighteenth century, some critics have concentrated
on Robert Challe as a prime source for the novel.[12] There are in
fact striking parallels between Challe's *Les Illustres Françaises*

and the narrative forms implemented by Prévost and Marivaux. I did not incude Challe in this work, however, because I found no direct support for the belief in his influence among the major authors' writings.

Aside from the common points illustrated by the example of *La Vie de Marianne,* the French novelists from Montesquieu to Sade do not reveal any unified patterns of development. They were individualists; but each was concerned with the struggle to add some dignity to the selected form. The novelists examined demonstrate seriousness toward the novel. A writer would not impose upon himself or his reader long discourses concerning the authenticity of his work, if he did not seek to be taken seriously. Similarly, writers would not have devoted so much energy in condemning *les romans* if they had not been concerned with improving the public concept toward their own creations. These are some of the reasons which justify the work at hand.

The transformation of the novel into a technically respectable genre at the end of the eighteenth century was visible in the texts as early as 1730. Even after 1784, however, the genre struggled for prestige in the eyes of critics, and it is still struggling today. The authors of the French *nouveau roman* express a profound disdain for the established notion of *le roman.* Although they would certainly reject the analogy, their search for innovative narrative means is not that different from the efforts of eighteenth-century writers.

NOTES

[1]Gustave Lanson, *Histoire de la littérature française* (Paris: Hachette, 1906), 659.

[2]Roger Laufer, *Style rococo, style des lumières* (Paris' Corti, 1965), 19.

[3]Daniel Mornet, *La Pensée française au XVIIIe siècle,* (Paris: Colin, 1965), 12.

[4]Boileau, *Art poétique,* Chant III, v. 119-21 (my translation).

[5]Voltaire, *Essai sur la poésie épique* (1733) (my translation).

[6]Diderot, *L'Eloge de Richardson,* in *OEuvres,* ed. André Billy (Paris: Gallimard, 1951), 1059 (my translation).

[7]Georges May, *Le Dilemme du roman au XVIIIe siècle* (Paris: Presses universitaires de France, 1963), chapter V.

[8]May, 184-85.

[9]Laclos, "Sur le roman de: *Cecilia,*" (1784).

[10]*Idem.*

[11]E. M. Forster, *Aspects of the Novel* (New York: Harcourt, Brace and World, 1927), 6. The reference is actually from Abel Chevally's *Le Roman anglais de notre temps.*

[12]See, for example, Lawrence J. Forno, "Robert Challe and the Eighteenth Century," in *Studies on Voltaire and the Eighteenth Century,* 79 (1971), 163-75.

II
MONTESQUIEU: A "SORT OF NOVEL"

Montesquieu was not the first French novelist of the eighteenth century, nor is he known to posterity as a novelist. His fame resides mainly in his role as a historian, in particular *L'Esprit des lois* (1748) and his *Considérations sur les causes de la grandeur des Romains et de leur décadence* (1732-48).

His contributions as a theoretician of law and chronicler do not however dismiss his fictional work. He began his career with a "sort of novel," *Les Lettres persanes* (1721), and ended it with an esthetic work, *L'Essai sur le goût* (1757). In the meantime, he demonstrated further interest in fiction with *Le Temple de Gnide* (1725) and *L'Histoire véritable* (1738).

Obviously, Montesquieu's career as an artist cannot be stressed extensively. His "Pensées," a sort of diary, reveal even more that his interests resided primarily in history. As a critic of the eighteenth-century novel, his ideas are relatively meager, since he wrote and lived earlier than the other novelists to be examined. The fictional interest of his own *Lettres persanes* is questioned by critics.[1] The novel itself is laden with reservations by its author as to whether it was a novel at all.

But Montesquieu did provide some remarks on the idea of *le roman* in 1721 and in later years; he discussed and respected certain conventions that were to become standard in the novel of the Enlightenment. These ideas are found in the two prefaces to *Les Lettres persanes*, and references to *les romans* in the novel and in Montesquieu's "Pensées."

The first preface to *Les Lettres persanes*, that of the original edition (see Appendix I), shows that Montesquieu was aware of conventions in the novel. In 1721, fictional conventions were a rather new discovery in France, and Montesquieu exploited most of them to the fullest. In this preface the reader supposedly learns of the book's conception, and the role of its anonymous "author": "But it is on the condition that I remain anonymous; for as soon as my name is known, I shall fall silent."

If Montesquieu accepted anonymity as a convention for fiction, he rejected another, that of the *dedication,* claiming that he would assume total responsibility for the book's acceptance. Aside from the satirical import of this claimed independence, the author's social position and personal fortune were sufficient to free him from any indebtedness to a sponsor or protector.

Another convention in fiction in the eighteenth century was the claim of *authenticity;* this pretention was echoed in the French Enlightenment novel to the point of insistence. Accordingly, Montesquieu presented his work as being a real one: "The Persians who write in this work stayed with me; we spent our lives together." Part of the satire of *Les Lettres persanes* resides in the narrative point of view; and Montesquieu did not dupe his contemporary reader any more than the modern one. There were nonetheless some Persians who travelled in France in the eighteenth century, as indicated, for example, by the arrival of the Persian ambassador in the ninety-first Persian letter. But when we are told that the author's Persians lived with him and totally confided in him, our skepticism is aroused.

Among the conventions in fiction discussed by Montesquieu in his first preface was the prefatory usage itself: "According to tradition, any translator. . .may embellish the front of his edition or gloss with a panegyric of the original, and denote its utility, its merit and excellence." A preface is a rather innocuous document, one that the reader may be tempted to overlook. And Montesquieu's nonchalance in this original preface would tend to justify such treatment. But he would assume a much more serious posture thirty-three years later.

The second preface to Montesquieu's novel, "Quelques Réflexions sur *Les Lettres persanes,*" was published with the text for the first time in the 1754 edition (see Appendix II). The text is crucial to Montesquieu's notion of the novel; it contains the principal tenets of his argument for the presence of a novel in *Les Lettres persanes,* as well as its subtle arrangement or "secret chain."

> Nothing pleased more in the *Persian Letters* than to find, without expecting to, a sort of novel. The reader can see its beginning, the development and the end. The diverse characters are placed in a chain which connects them together. To the degree that they stay in Europe, the customs of this part of the world appear to them as being less marvelous and less strange, and they are more or less struck by these marvelous and strange aspects, according to the differences of their personalities. (Appendix II)

Indeed, Montesquieu's first and most significant fictional creation is normally considered as pure satire, that is, the indirect criticism of French life and customs by means of the Persians. The first sentence from the 1754 preface (quoted above) seems to stress the satirical aspect of the work, while making allowance for the "novel" aspect.

Yet the work also contains thirty-three letters concerning life in Persia, and it is extremely likely that the "secret chain" mentioned by the author is the fictional or Persian element of the work. *Les Lettres persanes* begins with a view of life in Persia; the author refers frequently to the harem throughout the text, at strategic points, and concludes with a crisis not in France, but Persia. Those who are familiar with the "Quelques Réflexions" of 1754, as opposed to the readers of the 1721 edition, are also made aware of the inverse proportion of decreasing perplexity by Usbek and Rica, when confronted with European customs, while the furor increases back home in the seraglio.

It is thus apparent that the harem episode in *Les Lettres persanes* was more than a mere pretext for the satirical part of the work. After the initial contact with the Persians, layers of information on the East are periodically inserted. The two levels, fictional and satirical, then converge in Letters 146 and 147, where Usbek's tyranny toward his wives becomes implicitly analogous with the tyranny of the King of France toward his subjects.

The dual narrative purpose of *Les Lettres persanes* appears to be summarized by the "translator" himself; in Letter 11, the first of the celebrated letters on the Troglodyte nation, Usbek introduces the episode to Mirza in the following subtle manner: "There are certain truths which cannot really be taught, but which must be felt. Moral truths are such. Perhaps this bit of history will move you more than any subtle philosophy."

Les Lettres persanes, a "kind of novel," is also a kind of *letter novel.* Epistolary fiction was another eighteenth-century convention which Montesquieu controlled with a good deal of skill. The letter form lends a new dimension to fiction, one that is unequaled in most other narrative modes.[2] It permits multiple and simultaneous points of view, also referred to as the chamber of mirrors effect. The reader of epistolary fiction is given the impression that the characters are living and discovering their lives at the same time as the reader, even more so than with the first person narration. Also, it would be difficult to imagine a genre which was better suited to Montesquieu's ultimate intention, that of "being able to include some philosophy, some politics and some ethics in a novel, and to connect all of it by a secret and somewhat unrecognized chain" ("Quelques Réflexions sur les *Lettres persanes*").

The epistolary genre, which was to reach its artistic perfection in France with *Les Liaisons dangereuses* (1782), was not discovered by Montesquieu. Yet he was aware of its living dimension when he stated:

> Moreover, these types of novel are usually successful, because the people involved account for their own present situation, and this makes their passions felt more than all of the impersonal narrations which could be written on them. This is also the reason for the success of a few delightful works which have appeared since the *Persian Letters.*

Like any good author of epistolary fiction, Montesquieu delegates a large amount of responsibility to his characters; each time they take up their pens, they become more or less accountable for their manners of expression and actions, in contrast with the more detached and impersonal third-person mode.

Montesquieu was equally aware of the impromptu aspect of the letter-novel, when he remarked that the "actors" of his drama are not previously selected, and that no prior-established plan or intent exists in the mind of the "translator." He would have us believe that the work composed itself, letter by letter, and that numerous other conclusions were also imaginable.

The difference between the two prefaces to *Les Lettres persanes* is then striking. Both are important to the work; but if Montesquieu was aware of the nature of *Les Lettres persanes* in 1721, he did not reveal its subtle arrangement until 1754. As a novelist, he followed the serious and traditional approach of authenticity in 1721; in "Quelques Réflexions sur les *Lettres persanes*," he viewed the work as a "sort of novel." The reservation is serious in itself, since the pejorative idea of novel remained in France until the end of the century and beyond.

Montesquieu's reservations concerning the novel expressed in his 1754 preface are reinforced in the text itself. Whereas *Les Lettres persanes* provides a great wealth of sociological information spanning politics, religion, and mores of widely varying societies, it also contains remarks on the writing profession. In addition to highly unfavorable portraits of novelette writers (Letter 130), and books in general (135), the Persians inform us that a poet is "a grotesque member of the human race" (48), that critics are boring and prejudiced, and that writers of novels are "a type of poets who shock both the language of the mind and that of the heart; they spend their lives seeking nature and always fail to find it, and their characters are just as bizarre as winged dragons and sea monsters" (137).

Rica's visit to the *Bibliothèque de Saint-Victor* (Letter 137) was the occasion for another of Montesquieu's diatribes on the novel:

> I have seen, I said to him, some of your novels, and, if you saw ours, you would be even more shocked. They are so unnatural and embarrassing to our customs; ten years of passion are required before a suitor is permitted to see his lover's face. Still, authors are forced to lead their readers through boring preliminary documents. It is impossible that there be any variation of events. They depend on artifices which are even worse than the wrong that they would correct. I am sure that you would not find it acceptable that a sorceress would have an army rise up from the underground, and that one single hero would destroy one hundred thousand members of it. But such are our novels. The impersonal and oft-repeated

> adventures bore us, and these excessive marvels arouse our
> indignation. (Letter 137)

Rica's remarks are more general than one might believe; his
condemnation of the extravagant, the supernatural and the
impossible have direct bearing on the concept of the novel in
France in 1721. The novels of La Calprenède and Mlle de
Scudéry fitted Rica's definition much better than *Manon Lescaut*
or *Les Egarements du coeur et de l'esprit.* Ten years later, both
Prévost and Crébillon *fils* condemned *les romans* for the same
excesses, and in very similar terms.

Concerning Prévost, it should be pointed out that
Montesquieu had a rather marked dislike for *Manon Lescaut,*
which he read in 1734. Montesquieu rejected Manon as being a
"catin" and Des Grieux as a "fripon."[3] He did account for the
popularity of Prévost's novel, however, as having been due to
the love story in the novel, which in the public eye, excused all
other weaknesses. Love was in fact one of the basic ingredients
of the eighteenth-century French novel, and Montesquieu's evolution in taste, away from adventure and toward intrigue, follows
the more general evolution of the novel.

The following "pensée" provides Montesquieu's position
on the moral utility of the novel, a problem that beset the majority of French authors in the eighteenth century:

> The reading of novels is surely dangerous. Yet what is not
> dangerous? If only we had nothing else to correct than
> the ill effects of reading novels. But to order an ever-
> sensitive person not to have any emotions; to outlaw pas-
> sions, without even allowing for their rectification; to
> propose perfection to a century which becomes worse
> day by day; amid so much wickedness, to revolt against
> weakness, I truly fear that such lofty morals might be-
> come speculative, and that, when we are shown from so
> far away what we should be like, we are left as we are.[4]

Although this statement is relatively isolated in Montesquieu's
"Pensées," it is nonetheless a poignant observation on the novel.
The "dangerous" aspect of reading novels is very general, and
more likely refers to the treatment of love in the novel of the
preceding century, than to any specific impropriety. The state-

ment is written in the same perspective as the reproaches of extravagance in Letter 137 of *Les Lettres persanes;* Montesquieu was more interested in correcting the notion of novel of the past century than in establishing criteria for the genre in his own time. The mere fact that he acknowledged the potentiality of the novel as a means of controlling passion is quite progressive, and the majority of French novelists who followed him echoed the same call for moral reform.

In Montesquieu's *Essai sur le goût* (1757), there is only one passage which treats the novel specifically. Under the rubric "Des Plaisirs de la variété," he attempted to explain the pleasures afforded by the particular literary genres:

> It is thus that histories are pleasing to us by the variety of the narrations, novels by the variety of their prodigies, dramas by the variety of passions. . . . A prolonged uniformity renders all things unbearable; the same order of periods overwhelms us in a speech; the same numbers and the same misfortunes induce boredom in a long poem.[5]

The trivial, if not denunciatory context in which Montesquieu accounts for the novel should not be surprising. This unfavorable treatment of the genre by the very authors who practised it would persist until Choderlos de Laclos' discussion of fiction in the 1780 decade. Montesquieu's call for contrast and variety in the novel had already been stated in the 1754 "Réflexions," in his final instructions to the reader: "The reader is implored to remember that the main pleasure resided in the perpetual contrast between real things and the strange, novel or bizarre manner in which they were perceived."

Modern criticism could not have provided a better epilogue to *Les Lettres persanes.* The juxtaposition and contrast of the two radically different worlds, in which the strong and weak points of each are elicited, is the essence of Montesquieu's artistic process.

Montesquieu's literary observations, few as they may be, reveal a novelist conscious of his craft. Although his personal interests prevented him from providing a more detailed account of his concept of fiction, his remarks on the novel, whether satirical, as in 1721, or serious, as in his "Pensées," are informative as to what a *novel* was in 1721 and in later years. There is also a *novel* in *Les Lettres persanes,* however hidden or supposedly unintentional. It may have been dangerous, as were all novels, according to its author; but it was also the basic device for satirizing the decadence of France in the eighteenth century.

NOTES

[1]Those critics who argue against the presence of a novel in *Les Lettres persanes* are Antoine Adam (Introduction to *Les Lettres persanes* [Geneva: Droz, 1954]), and F. C. Green, ("Montesquieu the Novelist and Some Imitations of the *Lettres persanes*," *Modern Language Review*, 20, 32-42). Those critics who consider primarily the fictional aspect of the work are Roger Laufer, in "La Réussite romanesque et la signification des *Lettres persanes* de Montesquieu," *RHL*, 61 (1961), 188-203; Roger Mercier, in "Le Roman dans les *Lettres persanes*: structure et signification," *Revue des Sciences humaines*, 108 (1962), 345-56; and Richard L. Frautschi, "The Would-be Invisible Chain of *Les Lettres persanes*," *French Review*, 34 (1967), 604-12.

[2]For an excellent discussion of the potentiality of epistolary fiction, see Jean Rousset, *Forme et signification* (Paris: Corti, 1962).

[3]*OEuvres complètes de Montesquieu* (Paris: Gallimard, 1949), Vol. I, 1253.

[4]My translation is based on the Gallimard edition of Montesquieu's *OEuvres complètes*, I, 998.

[5]My translation is again based on the Gallimard edition of *OEuvres complètes*, II, 1245-46.

MONTESQUIEU: APPENDIX I
PREFACE (1721)

This is not a dedicatory epistle; and I seek no sponsorship for this book; it will be read, if it is good. And if it is bad, I do not care that it be read.

I have extracted these first letters to test the public's reaction; I have many more in my portfolio that I can provide in the future.

But it is on the condition that I remain anonymous; for as soon as my name is known, I shall fall silent. I know a woman who walks quite well, but who begins to limp as soon as people watch her. There are enough weaknesses in this work without being criticized for those of my own personality. If people knew my identity, they would say: "His book clashes with his character; he should spend his time at something better; this is not befitting a serious man." Critics never fail to provide this sort of observation, because they are able to provide them without excessive use of their minds.

The Persians who write in this work stayed with me; we spent our lives together. Since they looked on me as a man from a totally different world, they concealed nothing from me. In fact, people brought here from so far away could not keep their secrets forever. They shared with me the majority of their letters; I copied them. I have discovered some others which they surely would not have confided to me, so mortifying they were to their vanity and jealousy.

Thus my role is merely that of translator: all my efforts were aimed at adapting the work to our culture. I have spared the reader the Persian idiom as much as I could, and have saved him from an infinity of sublime expressions which would have bored him to death.

But that is not all I have done for him. I have removed the lengthy salutations and greetings with which the Orientals are just as lavish as we are, and I have omitted an infinite number of trivia which would not bear up to the test of truth, and which should disappear among friends.

If the majority of those who have written collections of letters had done the same, they would have seen their works dissipate into nothingness.

One thing has often surprised me: it is to see these Persians sometimes as well informed as myself about the customs and manners of this nation, to the point of being familiar with the slightest details, and to have noticed things which have been overlooked by many Gemans travelling in France, I am sure. I attribute this to the length of their stay here; besides, it is easier for an Asian to learn more about French customs in one year, than it is for a Frenchman to familiarize himself with Asian customs in four years, since the one group is so open, and the other so secretive.

According to tradition, any translator—or even the crudest commentator—may embellish the front of his edition or gloss with a panegyric of the original, and denote its utility, its merit and excellence. I have not done this, for obvious reasons. One of the best reasons is that it would be a very boring thing, placed in a location which is very boring in itself—that is, in a Preface.

MONTESQUIEU: APPENDIX II
"QUELQUES REFLEXIONS SUR LES *LETTRES PERSANES*"
(1754)

Nothing pleased more in the *Persian Letters* than to find, without expecting to, a sort of novel. The reader can see its beginning, the development and the end. The diverse characters are placed in a chain which connects them together. To the degree that they stay in Europe, the customs of this part of the world appear to them as being less marvelous and less strange, and they are more or less struck by these marvelous and strange aspects, according to the differences of their personalities. On the other hand, the anarchy increases in the Asian harem in proportion to the length of Usbek's absence, that is, in direct proportion to the increase of furor and the decrease of love in the seraglio.

Moreover, these types of novel are usually successful, because the people involved account for their own present situation, and this makes their passions felt more than all of the impersonal narrations which could be written on them. This is also the reason for the success of a few delightful works which have appeared since the *Persian Letters.*

Finally, in ordinary novels, digressions are not admissible except when they form an entirely separate story. One could not insert arguments, since none of the characters was brought in for the purpose of argument, and that would shock the nature and the purpose of the work. But in the epistolary form, where the actors are not pre-selected, and where the subjects treated are not dependent on any purpose or prior-established plan, the author gives himself the advantage of being able to include some philosophy, some politics and some ethics in a novel, and to connect all of it by a secret and somewhat unrecognized chain.

At first, the *Persian Letters* were such a great success that the booksellers tried everything to obtain sequels of it. They stopped everyone they met and asked: "Sir, I beg of you, write some more *Persian Letters* for me."

But what I have just said suffices to make people see that the work does not lend itself to any sequel, even less to any mixture with letters written by another, however ingenious these may be.

There are some traits which many people found too daring; but those people are asked to recall the general nature of this work. The Persians who were to play such a major role in it were suddenly transported to Europe, that is, into another universe. It was necessary that, for a time, they be portrayed full of ignorance and prejudice; the main preoccupation was to portray the germination and the development of their ideas. Their first reactions were of necessity peculiar; it appeared that they only had to be given that sort of peculiarity which coincides with wit; one only had to describe the feeling they had when confronted with each extraordinary thing. Far from purposely involving any aspect of our religion, not even imprudence was suspected. These points are continously combined with the sentiment of surprise and amazement, and not at all with the notion of investigation, even less with that of criticism. In speaking of our religion, these Persians were not supposed to appear any more informed than when they spoke of our customs and practices, and if they sometimes found our dogmas to be strange, this strangeness is clearly marked with their complete ignorance as to the relations which exist between these dogmas and our other credences.

This clarification is provided out of love for these great truths, aside from the normal respect for the human race, which the author did not wish to hurt in its most tender area. The reader is therefore requested to always regard the traits which I speak of as the result of surprise of people duly surprised, or as paradoxes posed by men who were not at all able to pose any. The reader is implored to remember that the main pleasure resided in the perpetual contrast between real things and the strange, novel or bizarre manner in which they were perceived. Assuredly, the nature and intent of the *Persian Letters* are so obvious that they will never dupe anyone except those who choose to dupe themselves.

III
MARIVAUX: TOWARD REALISM

Marivaux's ideas on the novel are almost impossible to present in unified form. Similar to Prévost and Diderot, he practiced literary criticism in periodical journals; he was a dramatist; and his own works of prose fiction demonstrate great variety and experimentation.[1]

Marivaux's early works of fiction, written from 1712 till 1714, were mainly parodies of the *romans précieux* of the seventeenth century. He then moved away from the novel and turned toward journalism, with articles written for *Le Mercure* (1717-1720), *Le Spectateur français* (1722-1724), and *Le Cabinet du philosophe* (1734-1735). Marivaux is best known for two novels; Part I of *La Vie de Marianne* appeared in 1731, Part II in 1734. This work was then abandoned in favor of *Le Paysan parvenu*, of which the five authentic parts appeared from May, 1734 until April, 1735. *La Vie de Marianne* was then resumed, with Parts II through VIII completed by July, 1738, and Parts IX to XI finished in 1742. The intermingling of journalistic essays with his major works of prose fiction is important, because the ideas expressed in the former elucidate considerably the definitive form of the latter.[2]

Recent criticism of Marivaux has concentrated on Marivaux's "early" novels as sources of information and explanations of his two masterpieces. Rosbottom's *Marivaux's Novels: Theme and Function in Early Eighteenth-Century Narrative* is one example.[3] I cannot totally share the enthusiasm expressed by others for the importance of these early texts. For me, they were parodies of serious novels, and not models to be imitated.

These early novels were: *Les Aventures de ***, ou les Effets surprenants de la sympathie* (1712), *Pharsamon, ou les Nouvelles Folies romanesques* (1713), *Le Bilboquet* (1713), *La*

Voiture embourbée (1713-1714), and *Le Télémaque travesti*
(1714).   The second text, *Pharsamon*, illustrates Marivaux's
concept of the "traditional" novel.   The principal sources for
this parody were Cervantes, especially concerning the relationship of the dubious master and cowardly valet, and Scarron's
Roman comique.   It would appear that Marivaux took the
least flattering elements of the two and mingled them in his
text.

All four of the main characters of *Pharsamon* owe most of
their woes to an excessive amount of reading novels, as witnessed
in the very first page:

> The old romances, the Amadis de Gaule, the Ariostos, and
> so many other books seemed to him to be the best suited
> lessons and those most able to give to his nephew that
> noble idea that he should have of fine love and glory
> (p. 393).

Similarly, the young maiden Cidalise talks with words "which
approached those that should be spoken by the heroine of a
novel" (p. 397).   And when the hero Pharsamon had been
wounded in a duel, Cidalise "uttered a sigh which could have
been taken for a yell; she was not yet accustomed to sighing like
a heroine of fiction" (p. 409).   It is difficult to find two successive pages in *Pharsamon* which do not contain some denunciation
of the novel, either by explicit reference or by parodied adventure.   Cidalise's mother, Dame Marguerite, attributes all of her
daughter's extravagances to the reading of bad books, i.e., novels:
"a thousand times novels had been thrown out through the win-
dow, but Cidalise had always found the secret of obtaining
others" (pp. 420-21).   In similar fashion, Pharsamon's uncle, M.
de la Méry, pinpoints the same source for his nephew's melan-
cholic behavior:

> So you admit that it was the volumes of novels which
> troubled your mind?   Give them to me—all of them.   Per-
> haps you would still want to read them; let me burn them;
> consider them as a dangerous pitfall, to which you have
> already succumbed; alas, I did not know that novels could
> produce such effects (p. 446).

M. de la Méry's advice went unheeded, however, since Pharsamon immediately resumes his *folies romanesques.*

At this early date, Marivaux demonstrated an extreme sensitivity to criticism of his work by others. In the "Avis au lecteur" of *Les Effets surprenants de la sympathie,* to which Deloffre has devoted an entire article,[4] Marivaux invites these potential critics to consider the work as that of a young man, but one with common sense, and not to expect to find a "correct" work of imitation. He also states that his work was above their "sterile laws for art" (p. 3), and that the human heart should be the prime criterion for judgment. Concerning the relationship between truth and art, he readily admits that this work was false by definition, and, like Diderot in *L'Eloge de Richardson,* remarked that sensitivity should be the dominant concern of the author.

The same "Avis au lecteur" contains one further point of interest for his later works, and one which serves to explain the abundance of digressions and reflections in *Le Paysan parvenu* and particularly in *La Vie de Marianne:*

> In my opinion, I have found that novels have been stripped of everything which could make them useful, and often times even entertaining. Those which are being composed at present are no more than simple adventures related with a haste which truly amuses the reader, but which does not move him or touch him. . . . The author of the ones which I present did not apparently share this preference, for his novel is interspersed with reflections which were found most interesting by some people to whom I read the manuscript (pp. 8-9).

Digressions were to be the very essence of *La Vie de Marianne.* They are the opportunity for the novelist to proffer his moral ideas, to expound philosophically on human behavior, and thus give his work a greater aura of respectability. In earlier adventure tales, "digressions" were merely superfluous sub-plots intended for entertainment; after Marivaux, they were transformed into an asset for the novelist.

One final remark about the structure of Marivaux's early works is in order. *La Voiture embourbée* poses the same problem of generic complexity that was encountered in *Pharsamon*

and *Les Effets surprenants de la sympathie.* It is another parody
of the novel, with elements of the impromptu, the travelogue
and farce. The same nihilistic attitude toward the genre is displayed: "Well, reader, you must know that in providing this
story to you, I am not so vain as to think that I am offering
you anything refined" (p. 314). *La Voiture embourbée* is also
rich in denunciations by the main characters of themselves and
of other fictional characters. But the text is not as impromptu
as Marivaux might have it appear: the incident of the quagmired
carriage not only sets the stage for the improvisation of a novel;
it also contains a narrative related in unusually realistic style.
The coachmen employ a style which one would expect from
coachmen, with the corresponding curses, interjections and
epithets.[5] It would seem that Marivaux had no fixed concept,
at least a positive one, of the constituent elements of the novel
in 1714. However, he proved himself most capable of masterful realist style, which was to become one of the strongest
assets of *Le Paysan parvenu.*

There are numerous analogies to be drawn between Marivaux's two major novels, analogies which are easy to understand
since the two were virtual contemporaries, *La Vie de Marianne* is
much longer than *Le Paysan parvenu,* almost three times as long
in fact, but both plots are relatively uncomplicated. Both central characters are forced to create a place for themselves in the
world, and both texts remained unfinished by their author.

La Vie de Marianne best demonstrates what constituted a
conventional novel in mid-eighteenth-century France. It was presented by its author as being an authentic, credible story. Marivaux exerted himself more than any other author in validating
his "authentic" sources; he provided an editor, a discoverer of
the "manuscript," not to mention the "real" friend for whom it
was intended. We can conclude that a *good* eighteenth-century
French novel was presented as *fact, not fiction.* Even Laclos
descended to the convention of authenticity, although such a
respect for convention was inconsistent with his innovations in
the other aspects of the novel.

In conjunction with the authenticity convention, *La Vie de
Marianne* was written accordingly in the *first person,* that is,
the heroine narrated the adventures that she had lived and experienced. The narration in the first person, or "la narration

dans la bouche du héros," as Prévost defined it, further enhanced the credibility of the novel, since it emanated from the best possible source, the very person involved. Whether or not the memoir convention was intended to make the reader forget he was reading a novel, it nonetheless permitted a nearly total effacement of the author, in favor of an emotionally involved character.

Marivaux's longest and most regular novel is also a *love story.* Although Marianne's initiation into the world of love begins on a rather tense note, since she is pursued by the aged and undesirable Climal, her main goal in life is the pursuit of happiness with Valville. The progress and concern for love in the French novel, from the harem intrigue in *Les Lettres persanes* to Sade, is consistent.

Marianne's narration of her personal adventures permits us to observe yet another common characteristic of the French Enlightenment novel: *social criticism.* During her lengthy experiences, she encounters representatives of all levels of society: laundry women and coachmen, nuns, young and old men, middle and upper class members, with varying degrees of goodness. In short, the novel is a *tableau de la vie humaine.* Social observation, which was the foreground in *Les Lettres persanes,* persisted in the French novel. It would be specialized in some cases, e.g., *Les Egarements du coeur et de l'esprit, La Nouvelle Héloïse* and *Les Liaisons dangereuses;* in other cases, it would include different cultures (*Manon Lescaut*), or reduce itself to a particular social problem, as in *La Religieuse.* The eighteenth-century French novelists unanimously strived to present a particular or general social group in their works.

Marivaux's heroine also went to some length to observe, evaluate and decide for or against the actions and impressions made by her fellows, so much so, in fact, that the author was severely criticized for these interruptions by his contemporaries. For Marivaux, moral observations were the essence of the novel, as he explicitly stated in *Les Effets surprenants de la sympathie.* Whether the ideal of *plaire et instruire* was illustrated as frequently as in *La Vie de Marianne,* merely postulated in a preface, or deduced from the narrative, the French novelists were all *moralists.* The nuance given to the maxim by the Marquis de Sade was of course exceptional, and although the actual works may have betrayed so elevated an ideal, the theoretical commitment to morality in fiction remained intact. Social improvement of weaknesses by their exposure was moreover a fundamental trait of all literature of the Enlightenment.

Finally, Marivaux's Marianne devoted a considerable amount of time to criticism of the genre which she practised, as was the case with Marivaux's early novels: "This beginning seems to indicate that it is a novel; it is not such, however, that I am telling; I am relating the truth just as I learned it from those who raised me" (p. 10). Passing reference to novels may seem trivial; on the other hand, there should have been no need for such condemnations, if Marivaux had complete confidence in his convention of authenticity. But he apparently did not. In order to separate his new works from the *romans romanesques* and to further promote their acceptance, he frequently denounced *les romans* in the course of his narrations. We must conclude that something was definitely wrong with the concept of novels at the time.

La Vie de Marianne is therefore representative of the general tendencies of the French novel in the first part of the eighteenth century. These tendencies could also be called conventions; but, in 1734, they were discoveries, and had not yet been perfected. Such traits were under constant scrutiny, as will be seen in Crébillon's criticism of *La Vie de Marianne*.

Whereas *La Vie de Marianne* is a common denominator, *Le Paysan parvenu* is Marivaux's most "pure" work. It is as devoid of extraneous material as Crébillon's *Egarements du coeur et de l'esprit*. Instead of placing his emphasis on adventure, Marivaux concentrated on a more delicate aspect of the novel: its language. His periodical essays show that he paid an increasing amount of attention to the use of language, the difficulty of finding the precise words for expression of certain emotions or a particular situation. A partisan of the Moderns in the Quarrel of the Ancients and the Moderns, he noted that language adapted itself to social and intellectual needs, and did not adhere to fixed models or patterns:

> If there came to France a generation of men who had more mental finesse than was ever before found in France or elsewhere, new words and new signs would be required

to express the new ideas of which this generation would
be capable; the words which we have would not suffice,
even if the ideas they expressed would have some similarity with the newly acquired ideas.[6]

In *Le Paysan parvenu,* words are a substitute for action. For
Jacob, the upstart peasant, words are active agents. A particular choice of vocabulary could provide an entire dramatic dialogue, as occurs early in Part I, when Jacob arrives at the home
of his first patroness. A word introduced by one character is
seized upon by and qualified or elaborated on by another.[7]

None of the many prefaces of *La Vie de Marianne* nor that
of *Le Paysan parvenu* contain any substantial indication of
Marivaux's ideas on the novel. Part IV of the latter does contain
a unique passage which serves that purpose, and which is provided as an appendix. The scene in question is Marivaux's
counterattack on Crébillon's *Ecumoire* which had been published in 1734; Part IV of *Le Paysan* was officially approved in
September of that same year.[8] In the meantime, Parts I and II
of *La Vie de Marianne* had also appeared, and these were the
source of the dispute. Marivaux's Marianne was renowned for
her inability to organize her story coherently. Therefore in Book
III of *L'Ecumoire,* Crébillon introduced an absurd genie, "La
taupe Moustache" (a mole), who assumed the role of spiritual
adviser to the heroine Néadarné. The mole distinguishes herself
by a profound knowledge of matters concerning love, and a gift
of gab which irritated Prince Tanzaï:

Begin again what you have just said, interrupted Tanzaï,
I will be hanged if I understood one single syllable of it.
What is this language that you are speaking? The language
of the Isle of Babble, replied the Mole.[9]

The heroine Néadarné soon assimilated the digressive and spontaneous style of her mentor, and by inference, that of Marianne.
For Crébillon *fils,* reflections in *La Vie de Marianne* were so frequent that they caused the reader to lose sight of the main story:

If by chance an incident provides the opportunity for a
reflection, may it be given, but it should be short, it
should never efface the main point, and it should always
lead the reader's attention back to the story which is

being told to him; and let us do away especially with
this nuisance of showing off, which upsets the mind, and
eliminates its natural charm.   Well then, once and for
all, Taupe, my love, give us facts, and no more verbiage.[10]

Such was the nature of Crébillon's parody of *La Vie de Marianne.*
In the "Avertissement" to Part II of this work, Marivaux had already responded to objections against his too frequent observations and verbose style.   In Part IV of *Le Paysan,* he was more
specific, and provides us with precise ideas on the novel.   The
main characters in this masterpiece of literary criticism are a
young author, who represents Crébillon *fils;* le Chevalier de
Saint-Louis, i.e., Marivaux, who was asked to evaluate the
former's book; and Jacob; all three are travelling in a carriage to
Versailles.

Marivaux's method of attacking Crébillon is as interesting
as the principles he sets forth.   In 1734, Marivaux was forty-six
years old, Crébillon twenty-seven.   They were thus separated by
a generation, one in which Marivaux had achieved considerably
more than the young author of *L'Ecumoire.*   Consequently,
Marivaux was in a position to teach the younger writer a lesson,
and crushed him with politeness and with subtle reproaches (see
Appendix, fifth paragraph).

Crébillon's situation in 1734 was similar to Marivaux's in
1712, when he also was in search of the proper direction for his
work.   Marivaux pointed out structural weaknesses which could
have been equally applied to *Pharsamon* and *Les Effets surprenants de la sympathie.*   His advice to the young author
centered around two related points: morality in fiction, and
the role of the reader.   Concerning the first one, Marivaux's
spokesman noted that Crébillon's work was oriented excessively
toward the "senses" and not toward the mind (sixth paragraph).
In distinguishing between reality and fiction, Marivaux claimed
that eroticism is a fact of life, but is better suited in everyday
life than in fiction.   His reader, who is discriminate and tasteful,
does not seek the explicit or the crude in his fiction.

As was mentioned earlier, Marivaux was a moralist.   He
states at the beginning of *Le Paysan parvenu:* "The narration of
my adventures will not be without use to those who seek to instruct themselves" (p. 6).   There is of course a good amount of

sensuality in Jacob's memoirs, but it is presented discreetly and nobly.

Marivaux's controversy with Crébillon *fils* represents a summary of his treatment of prose fiction as of 1734. Crébillon apparently gained from this criticism, since his masterpiece of three years later, *Les Egarements du coeur et de l'esprit,* was much more polite and refined than *L'Ecumoire.* By that time, Crébillon had also become an advocate of morality in fiction. Whereas both authors commenced with loosely-structured frivolities, they emerged along the positive lines of the mature French novel.

NOTES

[1]Since Frédéric Deloffre has done the most and the best editing of Marivaux's works, I used his editions of them throughout. They are: *OEuvres de jeunesse* (Paris: Gallimard, 1972); *Le Paysan parvenu* (Paris: Garnier, 1969); *Journaux et oeuvres diverses de Marivaux* (Paris: Garnier, 1969); and *La Vie de Marianne* (Paris: Garnier, 1957). All parenthetical references are based on these editions.

[2]An example is the article "Du Style," in *Le Cabinet du Philosophe*, p. 383, in which Marivaux defends his unconventional style in *La Vie de Marianne*.

[3]Ronald C. Rosbottom, *Marivaux's Novels: Theme and Function in Early Eighteenth-Century Narrative* (Rutherford, N.J.: Fairleigh Dickinson University Press, 1974).

[4]Frédéric Deloffre, "Premières Idées de Marivaux sur l'art du roman," *Esprit Créateur,* 4 (Winter 1961), 178-183.

[5]See p. 320 of the edition cited.

[6]The article "Du Style," in *Le Cabinet du philosophe*, p. 383.

[7]Deloffre, *Une Préciosité nouvelle: Marivaux et le marivaudage*, p. 197.

[8]Deloffre's introduction to *Le Paysan parvenu*, p. lxxv.

[9]Crébillon *fils, L'Ecumoire* (London: n.p., 1779), II, 158.

[10]*L'Ecumoire*, 177-78.

MARIVAUX: APPENDIX
EXTRACT FROM PART IV OF
LE PAYSAN PARVENU (1735)

And you, sir (he was speaking to the young man), do you have business where we are going?

I am going there to see a lord to whom I recently gave a book which was just published, and of which I am the author, he said. Oh yes! replied the officer; it is the book we were talking of the other day, when we dined together. That is the one precisely, responded the young man. Have you read it, sir? he added.

Yes, I returned it yesterday to one of my friends who had loaned it to me, said the officer. Well, sir, tell me what you think of it, I beg you, replied the young man. What would you make of my opinion? said the officer; it would not decide anything, sir. And yet, said the other, pressing him on, how do you find it?

In truth, sir, I am hardly in a position to judge it, it is not a book for me, I am too old.

What do you mean, too old! replied the young man. Yes, said the other, I believe that at a very early age, one could find pleasure in reading it: everything is considered good at an age when one seeks only to laugh, and when one is so avid with joy that it is taken wherever it is found, but the rest of us greybeards, we are like those finicky tasters who are not tempted by crude dishes, and who are excited only by a meal when they are given delicate and well-selected dishes. Moreover, I did not see the purpose of your work, I know not what it is aimed at, nor what is its goal. One would say that you did not take the trouble of researching your ideas, but you simply took whatever notion came to you, and that is different; in the first situation, one must compose, delete, select; in the second, one takes what presents itself, however strange it may be, and something always does present itself; for I believe that the mind always furnishes something, be it good or bad.

In addition, if purely fictitious things can be curious, if they are pleasing by virtue of being freely invented, then your book should be popular; if not to the mind, then at least to the senses; but I still believe that you made an error therein, due to lack of experience, and without realizing that there is not great merit in interesting people by the latter means, and that you seemed to me to have enough power to succeed by other means, this being due in general to an insufficient acquaintance with readers, as opposed to the hope of touching them to any extent by that means. It is true, sir, that we are naturally licentious or, to put it in a better way, corrupt; but in cases concerning works of wit, that must not be taken literally, nor should we all be treated uniquely on that basis. A reader wants to be approached gently. As an author, would you want to bear the responsibility for his corruption? Proceed discretely at least, make it gradual, but do not push it (corruption) to its extreme.

Our reader does like depravity, however, but not extreme or excessive depravity; the latter forms are tolerable only in society, which diminishes their shock; they are in their proper place there only, and we forget them, because there we are more human than anywhere else; but not in a book where it (depravity) becomes dull, dirty and repulsive, due to the little amount of suitability it has to the tranquil condition of a reader.

It is true that our reader is human also, but he is then a man at rest, with some taste; he is discriminate, he expects that his mind will be amused, all the while seeking immorality, but honorably, by refined means, by decency.

All which I have said does not negate the fact that there are some attractive things in your book; indeed, I have noticed several of that type.

As far as your style is concerned, I do not find it at all bad, with the exception of an occasional digressive, loosely-structured, and by that confusing sentence, nay, awkward ones; this is apparently due to the fact that you did not sufficiently sort out your ideas, nor did you put them in any particular order. But you are merely beginning, sir, and this is a slight weakness which you will correct with further writing, as well as the one of criticizing others, and criticizing them above all with that carefree and jesting tone which you tried to have, and with that same self-confidence that you yourself would ridicule or be regretful of, the day when you shall be a bit more philosophical, and when you will have acquired a certain manner of thinking which will be more mature and more befitting of you. For you will have more wit than you now have, since I have seen some things from you which promise it; you will not be very concerned with those things you have had up till now; and you will scarcely be concerned with all those things that might be had; that, at least, is the case with those who have written the most, based on what they say.

Furthermore, I am discussing criticism only as I have seen it in your book, and which concerns one of the guests (and he named him) who was with us the day that we dined together, and I must confess that I was surprised to find fifty or sixty pages of your work aimed directly against him; in truth, I would have preferred, out of my regard for you that they had not been present in it.

But here we are at our destination, you asked for my opinion; I gave it to you as a man who admires your talent, and who wished to see you one day the object of as much discussion as was directed at the man of whom we speak. For all of that you will be perhaps a more adept person than he is; but you should at least give the impression of a man who seems to be worthy of something.

The officer ended with that, and I am recording his words just as I understood them then.

Our carriage then came to a halt, we stepped down, and each went his own way.

IV
PREVOST: HISTORY AND THE NOVEL

L'Abbé Antoine-François Prévost (1697-1763) comes very close to epitomizing the hack writer in the eighteenth century. Between the years 1730 and the end of his life, he produced dozens of volumes of novels, many of which had a quasi-historical foundation. A renegade priest who was forced to seek refuge from persecution in England, Prévost wrote for the most part to pay his debts. He is known today for one short masterpiece which stands apart from the rest of his copious production, *l'Histoire du Chevalier Des Grieux et de Manon Lescaut* (1731), usually referred to by the latter portion of the title only.[1]

Manon Lescaut was intended to be volume VII of Prévost's larger work, the *Mémoires et aventures d'un homme de qualité.* In the *Author's Preface* to this larger work, which follows as an appendix, there is an interesting definition of the novel; the work is referred to as "récit, histoire, narration, tableau, ouvrage, travail and traité." We would not expect an author of fiction to label his work as such, in the eighteenth century or in any other; yet his paraphrase of the novel and its confusion with other genres typifies Prévost's entire approach. In general, he made every effort to associate his works with *l'histoire,* and, by the same token, vigorously dissociated his works with *les romans;* as will be seen, he had quite clear notions of both genres.

The complete title of Prévost's best-known work, *l'Histoire du Chevalier Des Grieux et de Manon Lescaut,* is indicative of Prévost's ambiguity. The confusion is more evident in the titles of his other works of the 1740 decade: *Histoire d'une Greque moderne* (1740); *Histoire de Marguerite d'Anjou, reine d'Angleterre* (1740); *Campagnes philosophiques, ou Mémoires de M. de Montcal, aide de camp de M. le maréchal de Schomberg, contenant l'histoire de la guerre d'Irlande* (1741); *Mémoires pour servir à l'histoire de Malte, ou Histoire de la jeunesse du com-*

mandeur de *** (1741); and *Histoire de Guillaume le con-
quérant, duc de Normandie et roi d'Angleterre* (1742). In each
of these titles, the word *histoire* is present. Whereas *Manon
Lescaut* and *L'Histoire d'une Greque moderne* can be readily
identified as fictitious, things are not so clear in the remaining
works, especially in cases concerning known historical figures
such as William the Conqueror and Marguerite of Anjou. The
modern French word *histoire* encompasses both meanings of
history and *story;* assuming that the same ambiguity occurred
in Prévost's time, it must be admitted that he intentionally confused history and fiction. He was not alone in this situation:
the subtitle of Fielding's *Tom Jones* is the "History of a Found-
ling," and Fielding also referred to the "historical" content of
his novel: "It is by falling into fiction, therefore, that we generally offend against this rule, of deserting probability, which the
historian, if ever, quits, till he foresakes his character and com-
mences a writer of romance" (*Tom Jones,* Book VIII, ch. 1).

Prévost was very certain as to the true meaning of history
in the sense of chronicle; in the *Lettres de Mentor à un jeune
seigneur* (1760), he stated that history was concerned with
humanity in general, with the rise and fall of political regimes,
liberty, slavery, the growth of the arts and the sciences, and the
general betterment of the human condition.[2] In this definition,
he makes no allowance for the possibility of adulterating or
romanticizing history in order to make it more appealing. On
the contrary, Prévost's correct notion of history coincides
with the emphatic position granted to it in the Enlightenment
and the efforts undertaken to make it a precise science.

Another facet of the diverse career interests of l'abbé
Prévost was his endeavor in journalism. Between 1733 and 1740,
he edited and contributed significantly to a review, *Le Pour et
Contre.* In it, he promised viewpoints "on everything which
could interest the public, in matters of science, the arts, books,
authors, and so on, without any prejudice, and with offense to
no one."

Le Pour et Contre is the prime source for Prévost's ideas
on the novel. The following entry, from Volume II, no. XVI
(1733), under the title "Reflections on Novels," gives a concise
image of what he understood by them: "These pleasant fancies,
engendered by the human mind in one of those outbursts of

imagination, force it to depart from the true and the credible, and are instead concerned with excessively supernatural ideas, which carry it beyond its own limits."

The date of this remark (1733) deserves an explanation. At the time, Prévost had commenced very few of his own fictional works; also, the use of the word *roman* at the same period more often than not referred to the insipid romance tales and *romans précieux* of the preceding century, since few novels had been written in the Enlightenment.

Nonetheless, the same negativism is apparent in the rest of Prévost's essay:

> These compositions of magicians and giants, of amorous intrigues and combats, of lovers loved and forsaken, of heroines so wonderfully faithful, were the delight of all the back streets of this Kingdom for a long time, and the preoccupation of delicate writers. . . . I know that so many of these volumes contain basically nothing more than fantasies. The true, and consequently the useful, are banished from them. These enchantments, slain giants, huge armies dispersed by one single man, the mild-mannered heros, wandering heroines—all of them are revolting to a sound mind, which rejects them (*P. & C.*, I, 108).

The central problem in Prévost's rejection of *les romans* is their excess. What he sought in good works, on the other hand, was the *true* and the morally *useful*. It is also noteworthy that the latter requirement was dependent on the presence of the former; this provides an explanation as to the frequency of Prévost's novels with pseudo-historical references.

The other major account of what Prévost thought of the contemporary novel appeared in *Le Pour et Contre* six years later, in volume XVII, no. CCXXXVIII (1739). Occasioned by a recently published historical work, Prévost pursued his condemnation of the blending of two distinct genres: history and the novel:

> In truth, I cannot be too astonished by the liberty which our writers of novels grant themselves, when they trans-

> form into ridicule such great actions as these, which
> ought to inspire as much veneration as admiration. In
> general, the blending of history and fiction has always
> seemed reproachable to me. In a novel, everything
> should be fabricated. By what right can we permit dis-
> honor to the memory of people whose merits have caused
> history to perpetuate their names? What can be the rea-
> son for attributing to them weaknesses which will merely
> obscure their virtues?

In the original text, the reference to writers of novels ("faiseurs
de romans") is far from being a positive reference to the profession. Here a new requirement is imposed: "In a novel, everything should be fabricated." It underscores the inseparable gap
between what Prévost considered to be writing himself, and what
the known novelists of the period seemed to be writing. His observation is all the more ironic when one recalls the large
amounts of fiction which he composed in rapid succession.

Twenty years later, in a treatment of "Biography" in the
Lettres de Mentor à un jeune seigneur, Prévost differentiated
good novels from the bad:

> Thus it is that we find good novels to be more rare than
> good history; and this remark should not cause me to be
> suspected of wanting to recommend the reading of an
> infinite number of dull and obscene compositions, which
> are published under the title of novels and tales. The vice
> and excess with which they are filled can please no one
> but the corrupt, the lazy and the ignorant, and places
> them even below the level of contempt of a virtuous and
> sensible reader (see Appendix I).

There is considerable doubt as to the authenticity of the *Lettres
de Mentor à un jeune seigneur.*[3] And yet, the text is generally
in perfect agreement with Prévost's other ideas expressed at that
time. Prévost's attitude of 1730 toward the novel has been modified considerably because of the appearance of numerous progressive and artistic works in those years, and which have come
to be known as novels. In the same passage, he referred to excellence achieved in foreign novels. In his *Mémoires pour servir
à l'histoire de la vertu* (1762), he was more specific. The novels
of Samuel Richardson had caused a revolution in attitude toward

the novel, and Prévost, Diderot, and Rousseau praised Richardson, while denouncing their fellow French novelists.[4]

One of the main positive criteria which has filtered through Prévost's condemnations of the novel is the need for morality in it. Prévost was more adamant in this regard than any of his contemporaries. Whether in history, biography or the novel, Prévost defined the purpose of all good literature as the instruction of the public. The *Author's Preface* to *Manon Lescaut* is apropos in this regard; he promised that "the entire work is a moral treatise, pleasantly reduced into practice." He repeated this Horatian insistency on moral utility in the Preface to the *Doyen de Killerine*:

> But I have yet to name a motive which is infinitely more noble than the most noble of the other three, that is surely the only one capable of elevating an historian to the degree of perfection which would make people to look upon him as a model, and it is the desire to *make himself useful*. All is so neatly expressed in these three words, that they warrant no other commentary for those who grasp them (*O. C.*, vol. 8, p. xv).

The golden rule of moral utility has been revealed at last. *Manon Lescaut* is the French counterpart of Defoe's *Moll Flanders*, in that a young woman with some admirable qualities is exposed to the vicissitudes of contemporary society. It is far from being as salacious as some of the tales of Diderot and Crébillon, and yet one conservative critic, Montesquieu, denounced the work because of the immorality of the heroine.[5] Prévost's defense of the moral value of the work resides in the notion that the characters are victims of their fate (see Appendix I).

In still another preface ("Avant-Propos") to the *Doyen de Killerine*, Prévost noted that since truth itself would not always be enough to maintain the reader's attention, an author ("un historien") may be tempted to deviate from it: "Since truth alone does not always please, when one is interested in pleasing, it is not easy to remain within such narrow limits as these; the truth is disguised, if one cannot alter it; or it is elaborated and made agreeable" (*O. C.*, vol. 8, p. xiv). This observation shows the steady erosion of Prévost's absolute insistence on the true and the useful, as well as suggesting his hypocrisy. Gone is the total refusal of everything under the generic title of *novel.*

Prévost was aiming himself toward a middle position, between the historical genre and the ignominious romances. He did not find it until 1760. In the fourth of the *Lettres de Mentor,* entitled "Sur le Biographie," Prévost came quite close to a definition of his own methodology (see Appendix I). He refers to such works as "artificial" biography which, when executed well, are capable of instilling moral precepts. Although he had earlier claimed that everything should be fabricated in a novel, he allows here the possiblity of digression and expansion of an historical basis. Creative imagination has now replaced factual historical truth as the grounds for good works. There were then two levels of truth for Prévost: factual or historical truth, which serves as a point of departure for invented and artistic truth.

The fact that *Manon Lescaut* was presented as being one small part of the *Mémoires et aventures d'un homme de qualité* bears a further qualification. We have already mentioned the justification by Renoncour (the man of quality) as to why *Manon* was introduced separately. Prévost came closer to accounting for the effectiveness of the first person narrative used in this work than any of his contemporaries:

> May I not add, as proof of the interest which dominates
> in this type of writing, that the authors of the best novels
> have not imagined a more powerful method for entertain-
> ing and interesting, than to put their narration in the very
> mouth of their hero (Appendix I).

Similar to Marivaux's Marianne and Crébillon's Meilcour, the hero of the collective works of Prévost enjoys the vantage point of already having lived his adventures and of now being able to relate them.

The narration in the first person permits the "artificial biography" as is found here to rival with the letter novel in eighteenth-century France, in terms of the dynamics and the simultaneity of the recitation. It is here too that Prévost can in part justify the "biographical" element of his doctrine. Jean Rousset reminds us that by attributing the story to the characters, French novelists of the period were able to eclipse themselves and convey the impression that it was the hero who held the pen in hand.[6] In *Manon Lescaut,* Prévost took full advantage of the potentials of the first person convention. This effacement of the author is ideal for a writer who publicly expressed contempt for the genre of prose fiction.

Although it was designed to assure the maximum amount of credibility, the narration by the main character is not without its problems. Since *Manon* is only part of a much larger work, and since there is no real affinity between the two, the role of the man of quality becomes crucial. He does fix the proper perspective for the work by his observation early in the novel: "It is a young fool whom I have to portray, who would rather forego happiness in favor of intentionally rushing toward the most extreme of miseries." Elsewhere in the work, the man of quality is compelled to remind us of the basic circumstances of the narration. Midway through it, after Des Grieux has spoken for more than an hour, it is necessary to grant him a respite, after which he resumes his tragic "histoire." As Stewart says, Prévost tried to simultaneously maintain two fictions, that of the man of quality, and that of Des Grieux.[7]

The choice of the narration "in the hero's mouth" went beyond the mere adherence to conventions in the novel and the desire to entertain and instruct. Its ultimate purpose in the hands of Prévost is found in the *Lettres de Mentor:* ". . .an author who provides us with the story of an imaginary hero, but who fills it with grand and edifying adventures, causes us to forget that we are reading a novel, because of their realism" (Appendix I). This intent, stated very near the end of Prévost's career, is the culminating point in his oblique approach to the novel. The memoir convention, whether it was hidden behind *histoire* or any other mask, was more efficacious, according to Prévost, than any work known as a *roman.*

In spite of the reservation previously expressed concerning the authenticity of the *Lettres de Mentor,* one final observation is in order. Prévost remarked that "one can learn how the human heart allows itself to be guided" and that moral portraits "serve to prevent us from becoming fools." These remarks have important implications for the story of Des Grieux. The Jansenist point of view of helplessness and prior-established fate persists throughout des Grieux's narration. It is particularly visible in the reflexive verb patterns used by him ("Je me laissai conduire" and "Je me trouvai enflammé"). The extent of Des Crieux's awareness of this passivity is not clear, but he consistently presents himself to Renoncour as a victim of fate. The authentic eye-witness approach thus serves to place other witnesses (the readers) on their guard against similar dangers.

It is extremely unlikely that Prévost duped anyone into believing that his novels were something other than just that, and least of all himself. We know from one contemporary account that he was criticized for his contradictory method.[8] The choice of an ambiguous word such as *histoire* in Prévost's titles may seem insignificant, but it is fundamental in his case, since the proper term, *le roman,* was an anachronism. In place of the connotation of adventure tales, he sought a valid and reputable label for his more unified and coherent creations, and those of his contemporaries.

It was only in a rare moment of honesty, in several paragraphs in *Le Pour et Contre* in 1735, that Prévost revealed his basic strategy:

> I can be no more generous to a few works of the same type which I have composed at various times. Although there is not one from among them which does not have a great number of truths as its basis, I am forced to confess that, having wished to instill moral precepts in place of an agreeable narration, I added to them many things for which I require no other support than that of the imagination. . . . *Cleveland* and the *Doyen de Killerine,* whose second part is being prepared, are works totally useless for History, and whose merit consists in a worthy and entertaining story (P. & C., II, 94-95).

This "confession" contains what has been suspected throughout, i.e., that the definition of prose fiction was subordinated to the interests of entertaining and instructing. The example of Prévost serves to explain considerably the frequent condemnations of *les romans* by *les romanciers du dix-huitième siècle.* Concepts and definitions were simply not in pace with creativity in practice.

NOTES

[1]The edition of *Manon Lescaut* used is found in *Romanciers du XVIIIe sìcle,* vol. I (Paris: Gallimard, 1960). The preface of the novel used for my translation is also based on this edition. For Prévost's other works, I refer to *OEuvres choisies de Prévost* (Paris: Grabit, 1816), which is also the source for the first appendix, extracted from the *Lettres de Mentor à un jeune seigneur.* It is referred to as *O. C.* For *Le Pour et Contre,* I used the Slatkine Reprints edition (Geneva: 1967), and refer to it as *P. & C.*

[2]*O. C.,* vol. 34, pp. 226-27.

[3]According to Jean Sgard, in *Prévost romancier* (Paris: Corti, 1968), the text was a mere translation of an earlier English work (p. 566). According to Henri Harrisse, in his *Abbé Prévost* (Paris: Calmann Lévy, 1896), Prévost did indeed write the *Lettres de Mentor* (p. 415). The various editions of Prévost's works tend to agree with Sgard's opinion. As I stated earlier, however, the ideas contained in the text are in agreement with Prévost's other ideas as expressed in contemporary writings (e.g., his *Mémoires pour servir à l'histoire de la vertu*).

[4]For specific judgements on Richardson by Rousseau, Diderot and Laclos, and their relation to Prévost's own evolving thoughts, see my "Richardson's Influence on the Concept of the Novel in Eighteenth-Century France," in *Comparative Literature Studies,* vol. XIV, no. 3 (1977).

[5]Montesquieu, "Mes Pensées," in *OEuvres complètes* (Bibliothèque de la Pléiade), vol. I, p. 1253.

[6]Jean Rousset, "Prévost romancier: la forme autobiographique," in *Actes des Colloques d'Aix-en-Provence* (Presses universitaires d'Aix, 1965), p. 197.

[7]Philip Stewart, *Imitation and Illusion in the French Memoir Novel,* (New Haven, Conn.: Yale University Press, 1969), p. 116.

[8]The critic in question was Aubert de la Chesnaye des Bois. See Georges May, *Le Dilemme du roman au XVIIIe siècle* (Paris: Presses universitaires, 1963), p. 158.

PREVOST: APPENDIX I
EXTRACT FROM
LETTRES DE MENTOR A UN JEUNE SEIGNEUR (1760)

May I not add, as proof of the interest which dominates in this type of writing, that the authors of the best novels have not imagined a more powerful method for entertaining and interesting, than to put their narration in the very mouth of their hero.

The word novel, occasioned by this subject, provides me with the opportunity to observe that this sort of artificial biography has its advantages, when it is executed by the hand of a master. Aided by connections with historical truth, the author is free to select those events which he deems the fittest for the instillation of moral principles or any other type of instruction. The painter who depicts scenes which actually exist with a precise resemblance, is in possession of a praiseworthy art; but surely, he whose creative instrument, as is energetically expressed by the most imaginative of minds, excels in creating the most beautiful scenes inspired from within himself, and with the ability to adapt the fictitious to the truly natural, deserves acclaim both for his method and for his genius. Similarly, an author who provides us with the story of an imaginary hero, but who fills it with grand and edifying adventures, causes us to forget that we are reading a novel, because of their realism; (an author) who interests our passions and arouses all of the affections of the human heart, must be in possession of talent and genius which are worthy of great esteem. Thus it is that we find good novels to be more rare than good history; and this remark should not cause me to be suspected of wanting to recommend the reading of an infinite number of dull and obscene compositions, which are published under the title of novels and tales. The vice and excess with which they are filled can please no one but the corrupt, the lazy and the ignorant, and places them even below the level of contempt of a virtuous and sensible reader. But in foreign languages, as in our own, there are some of yet

another quality, in which one can learn how the human heart allows itself to be guided, but where one also finds good lessons of
use to everyone and excellent moral portraits, which serve to
prevent us from becoming fools, and by making us laugh at the
follies of others.

PREVOST: APPENDIX II
"AVIS DE L'AUTEUR" FROM
MEMOIRES D'UN HOMME DE QUALITE (1731)

Although I could have included in my memoirs the adventures of the Chevalier Des Grieux, it seemed to me that, without having any direct relationship, the reader would experience more satisfaction in finding them presented separately. A narration of this length would have excessively interrupted the thread of my own story. Far be it from my intention to claim to be an exact writer; I am aware however that a narration ought to be devoid of the details which could render it cumbersome and awkward. This is the principle of Horace:

> Ut jam nunc dicat jam nunc debentia dici,
> Pleraque differat, ac praesens in tempus omittat.
> (One should say in the beginning what is proper to the beginning, the rest should be delayed until its proper time occurs.)

There is no need for such a profound authority to prove so simple a truth, since common sense is the original source of this rule.

If the public has found anything pleasant or interesting in the story of my life, I venture to promise that there will be no less satisfaction with this supplement. In the conduct of Des Grieux, there will be seen a frightening example of the force of passion. It is a young fool whom I have to portray, who would rather forego happiness in favor of intentionally rushing toward the most extreme of miseries; with all the qualities that compose the highest esteem, he prefers to choose an obscure and vagabond life instead of all the advantages of good fortune and nature; he can foresee his troubles without wanting to avoid them; he feels them and is burdened by them, without profiting from the solutions incessantly offered and which could put an end to them at any moment; finally, he is of an obscure character, a blend of virtues and vices, a perpetual contrast of good intentions and wicked actions.   Such is the essence of the portrait that I present.   Persons of good sense will not consider a work of this type as useless.   Aside from a pleasant reading, it contains few events which would not contribute to moral instruction; and, in my opinion, a significant service is rendered to the public, when it is instructed and entertained.

One cannot reflect on moral principles without being surprised to see them kept in respect and neglect; and one wonders what is the reason for this peculiarity of the human mind, which causes it to taste the ideas of goodness and perfection, but which in reality alienate it.   If persons of a certain pattern of mind and refinement were to examine the most frequent of their conversation topics, even of their private dreams, it would be easy to see that they almost always revolve around moral considerations. The sweetest moments of their lives are those that, either alone or with a friend, they spend in a candid discussion of the charms of virtue, the comforts of friendship, the means of attaining happiness, or of natural weaknesses which keep us from it, and remedies which can cure those weaknesses.   Horace and Boileau refer to this type of conversation as one of the finest traits of their image of a happy life.   How then does it happen that we fall from such elevated aspirations and suddenly find ourselves on the common level of all men?   I am mistaken if the explanation which I am about to provide does not serve to resolve this contradiction between our ideas and our acts; since all moral precepts are merely vague and general principles, it is quite difficult to make a particular application of them to a point concerning morals and actions.   So let us put it into an example.   Noble people realize that mildness and humanitarianism are admirable virtues, and feel inclined to practice them; but do they remain so at the moment of application?   Is there no mistake as to the intended?   A hundred difficulties are imposed.   One has fear of becoming a dupe all the while attempting to be benevolent and generous; fear of being considered weak by the appearance of tenderness and sensitivity; in short, fear of exceeding or of not fulfilling obligations too obscurely wrapped in the general notions of humanity and kindness.   In the presence of the doubt, only experience or examples can reasonably determine the direction for the heart to follow.   Now experience is not an asset which all men can freely grant themselves; it depends on different situations in which men are placed by fortune. There remains only the example which can serve as a rule to many people in the exercise of virtue. It is precisely for this sort of reader that works like this one can be extremely useful, at least when they are written by a person of honor and good sense. Each fact reported in it is a ray of light, a piece of information which reinforces experience; each episode is a model one can imitate; all that is lacking is the adjustment to the circumstances in which one finds oneself. The entire work is a moral treatise, pleasantly reduced into practice.

The stern reader will perhaps be offended to see me take up my pen again at my age, in order to write tales of adventure and love; but if the explanation which I have just provided is sound, then it justifies men; if it is erroneous, then my error will constitute my apology.

V
CRÉBILLON *FILS:*
CONSTRUCTIVE CRITICISM FOR THE NOVEL

Crébillon *fils* (1707-1777) was by no means the most famous French novelist of the Enlightenment. Rather, he was an experimenter in fiction, having delved into the epistolary form with the *Lettres de la Marquise de M*** au comte de R**** (1732), and the *conte*, with *L'Ecumoire* (1734) and *Le Sopha* (1740) constituting the major ones. His most famous work, and the one which is most studied and commented in recent times is *Les Egarements du coeur et de l'esprit* (1736).

Several ironic incidents occurred in Crébillon's life which are symptomatic of the confused relationship between author and public at that time. In 1734, he was imprisoned at Vincennes for having authored the subversive *Ecumoire.* In 1742, he was banished from the region of Paris because of charges of immorality leveled against *Le Sopha.* But some years later, in 1759, he was appointed "censeur royal pour les belles-lettres," and so passing from the state of the prosecuted to that of prosecutor. This contradictory reversal of fortune is surely due to evolving trends, attitudes and different administrations; and yet it also bears on an evolution which the author himself experienced, and which was visible in the general progress of prose fiction.

Why did Crébillon *fils* encounter so much legal difficulty with his *contes?* The basic narrative situation in *Le Sopha* provides one explanation; in it, the author imagines a fictional device not unlike that found in Diderot's *Les Bijoux indiscrets.* As the title ("The Sofa") suggests, many of the episodes are related by Amanzéi, who had been metamorphosized into a sofa, and whose narrative sources are derived from his past contact with the most intimate areas of those women who graced him with their presence. When allusions to political and religious authorities of the time are included, it becomes quite clear why the author of *Le Sopha* experienced problems after its publication.

Le Sopha is of further interest to Crébillon's notion of what was the proper domain of fiction; few scenes in the tale pass without interruption by editorial comments on the nature of the *conte,* of fiction in general, and of the role of the author. It is here that Crébillon also confronts the problem of morality in fiction. Amanzéi insists on interjecting moral observations and judgments in his adventures, whereas his lord and main listener, the Sultan, objects to the point of threatening with the death penalty those who would dare offer such judgments. Crébillon was more ambiguous here than he had been in the Preface to *Les Egarements du coeur et de l'esprit;* he seemed to say that whatever an author's intent might be, a work of fiction would be considered insipid by an insipid reader, while it would be interpreted as informative by an enlightened reader.

Before the main source of Crébillon's esthetics of the novel is examined, a brief mention should be made of his experiment with the letter novel in 1732. *Les Lettres de la Marquise de M*** au comte de R**** is a curious epistolary work, in that only one side of the correspondence (the letters of the Marquise) is presented. Consequently she is compelled to "reconstruct" the letters from the count, with presuppositions, repetitions and references to the letters which are "absent." As in the case of *Les Egarements du coeur et de l'esprit,* the *Lettres de la Marquise* is basically a love story involving the initiation into mundane society of a young man by an older, more knowledgeable woman. Also, the earlier text, like the later one, contains occasional condemnations of the genre being practiced; the *Marquise* observes in Letter XVI:

> I have no doubt that this appears extraordinary to you;
> but whether novels have corrupted my mind in this in-
> stance, or whether I was instilled with this way of think-
> ing from birth, I do not see how what you are proposing
> to me is essential to my happiness.[1]

Thus Crébillon's first epistolary venture introduces most of the characteristics of his major work: a *love story,* presented as being *authentic memoirs,* but which are not totally convincing, since the narrator occasionally reminds us of the *danger of reading them.*

The publication of *Les Egarements du coeur et de l'esprit* in 1736 occurred at a critical moment in the evolution of the French novel. Works of fiction were obviously appearing regularly (Lesage, Marivaux and Prévost), while critical concepts of the genre had not advanced in the slightest degree. The novel was still being confused with the epic,[2] and French authors continued to publicly scorn it. Part I of *Les Egarements* appeared in 1736, and its Preface was included in that first publication. In this Preface, which is provided as an Appendix,[3] Crébillon goes beyond mere conventions and provides one of the most objective and far-reaching accounts of the novel's status to date. The first paragraph is in fact a break with convention, that of prefaces in themselves. As opposed to exaggerated promises of veracity and authenticity, he assigns to the reader the choice of interpreting the work as fact or fiction.

In the second paragraph of the Preface, the author confronts the more serious problem of the relation of morality and the novel. Although he was content to evade the issue in *Le Sopha,* in a totally different set of circumstances, there is no ambiguity here: "The man who writes can have but two aims: the useful and the agreeable." Although few authors had succeeded in combining the dual needs of Horaces's axiom *utile et dulci,* Crébillon sought to impose it as a rule, in view of the novel's reputation of being immoral. Indeed, most French novelists of the eighteenth century (Prévost and Rousseau are notable examples) promised both the useful and the pleasant. Even Laclos and Sade would cite this rule as a guide for others as well as for themselves to respect, although they are usually associated with the *libertinage* movement of the latter part of the century. The point of view of these two was radically different from that of the majority of other novelists; Laclos and Sade placed more emphasis on the portrayal of vice punished than virtue rewarded.

The following (third) paragraph of the Preface to *Les Egarements du coeur et de l'esprit* contains the most succinct elements of Crébillon's philosophy of the novel, and deserves a detailed commentary:

> The novel, so despised by sensible people, and often
> rightly so, would perhaps be the genre which could be
> rendered the most useful, if it were well managed, if,
> instead of filling it with somber and far-fetched stories,
> with heroes whose characters and adventures always sur-
> pass the limit of credibility, if it were made, like comedy,
> the tableau of human life, and if vice and excess were cen-
> sured in it.

Crébillon's statement is subdued by conditions and contingen-
cies. However, even a contingent allowance for the possibility
of the French novel to become the most useful genre, in terms
of moral effectiveness, is revolutionary. All reservations aside,
his statement announces a trend of positive thinking toward
the novel which would be fully realized at the end of the century. The uniqueness of Crébillon's favorable opinion here lies
in the analogy of the novel and comedy, and the basis for association of the two is the illusive notion of *verisimilitude,* which is
found in the comedy, according to the author, but absent in fiction.

French literature is characterized by rules and its adherence
to them. There are of course exceptions, and spectacular ones.
The observance of guidelines was particularly apparent in French
neoclassical literature in the period which immediately precedes
the age of Crébillon *fils.* The classically preferred genres were, at
least according to Boileau's *Art poétique,* the epic, the tragedy,
and the comedy, followed by other verse genres, and in that
order. There was no place for the novel, *le roman,* in this hierarchy, at least not a very dignified place (see Introduction).
On the other hand, the comedy had been firmly established in
France due to the works of Molière. The author of *Tartuffe,*
Le Misantrope, L'Avare and so many other masterpieces of
archetypal portrayals, had dared to enlarge and exaggerate vices,
so that they would become more visible and so that they could
be corrected. As opposed to tragedy, where only aristocratic
and elite strata of society were present, the comedy is the
"tableau of human life," that is, a valid representation of society
of the period. Although he dealt only with the higher levels of
a structured society in *Les Egarements,* he nonetheless provided
a wide tableau of members from that group: Versac, represent-
ing evil incarnate; Mme de Senanges, symbolizing debauchery
and vanity; youth and innocence, shown in the person of

Hortense de Théville; finally, social accomplishment and poise, portrayed in the role of Mme de Lursay.

Crébillon *fils* remained a *classique* by his association of comedy and the novel, and he was progressive in his efforts to lend dignity to the latter genre by borrowing support from the former. In view of these theoretical efforts, it comes as no surprise that the structure of *Les Egarements du coeur et de l'esprit* bears close resemblance to that of the classical French theater. Crébillon's greatest novel is devoid of heroic adventure; it is on the contrary, limited to verbal action. If the transitional days are excluded, only *twelve* days in Meilcour's life are actually presented, resulting in a time pattern which resembles the drama as much as the novel. Etiemble has even divided these twelve days into theatrical scenes, which further underscores the affinity between the two genres.[4]

The degree to which these theatrical conventions were intentionally imposed by Crébillon on his novel remains speculative. Yet further evidence for the novel-comedy association is found in his correspondence, in a letter to a friend and fellow writer, P. V. Besenval, who had sought Crébillon's advice on the manuscript of a novel entitled *Le Spleen;* the following is an excerpt from Crébillon's reaction:

> To succeed in this project, you will first have to arrange a sort of table of the different materials which you treat. You will ponder on all the subjects offered by the world to the prudent observer. You will then include them in a list, with a brief indication in the form of chapter synopses. When you feel that you have assembled the main topics and your list is complete, we will discuss it. Once these materials are organized, you will begin a second process, that is, assigning them a *natural order,* which will give rise to the successive parts, so that you do not treat in the beginning what would fare better if it were in the middle or at the end. *In a book, it is just like in a drama,* a generation of interrelated and connected things, which people call a beautiful harmony.[5]

This passage is important not only for the pursuit of the analogy between the comedy and the novel, but also because it gives a rare account of how a master novelist of the eighteenth century went about his composition. *Les Egarements du coeur et de l'esprit* does in fact possess a "natural order": the initial overtures made by Meilcour to Mme de Lursay; then his wanderings; finally, the closing of the plot's circle with his somewhat reluctant return to her.

In the fourth paragraph of this Preface, there is another lesson in creative composition, and one which is more concerned with the subject of this study. Crébillon states that if the novel were reformed according to his recommendations, then the reader "would no longer find in it those extraordinary and tragic events which carry away the imagination and which tear the heart in two; no more heroes who cross the sea only to be captured at a given point by Turks; no more intrigues in the harem . . .no more unexpected deaths; and far fewer subterranean adventures." Although no author is specifically named, the veiled references can be considered as an attack on the majority of French novels written prior to Crébillon's time. Some of his condemnations, e.g., "extraordinary and tragic events. . .which tear the heart in two" call to mind Prévost. The reference to intrigues in the harem applies quite accurately to Montesquieu, and Lesage is implicated by the reference to subterranean adventures. The only major figure absent from this list of abusers is Marivaux, and he would be denounced within the text of *Les Egarements*.[6]

In the remaining portion of this same fourth paragraph, Crébillon *fils* comes to terms with particular artistic norms for the novel. By the mention of the "event prepared with art and achieved naturally," he is implying that the novel, like any other creative mode, involves craft and artifice. The "natural" aspect is repeated several paragraphs further: "I know of nothing which should or which can prevent an author from extracting his characters and his portraits from the depths of nature." Crébillon's interpretation of nature is not at all that of Marivaux, who was interested in much less refined levels of society, nor that of the other "realist" artists of the period. And yet within his limited viewpoint, he is concerned with realistically portraying society, since all of the virtues and vices of the aristocracy are represented.

Finally, the mention of the need to see man such as he is (end of the fourth paragraph of the Preface, and repeated in the sixth paragraph) is further proof of Crébillon's modernism.

French literature prior to 1736 had placed the emphasis on portraying man such as he ought to be. The novel of the eighteenth century evolved on the contrary toward portraits of man as he really is. The works of Prévost and Marivaux provide excellent examples of eighteenth-century realism. Even though the milieu in *Les Egarements du coeur et de l'esprit* is elitist, it is a valid description of eighteenth-century libertine groups.

Crébillon *fils* was extremely ambitious in his efforts to reform popular attitude toward the novel; he said that he was willing to stand alone against those who would cling to the "ostentatious puerilities" of the old romances. In the same (fifth) paragraph, he recognized that tastes and attitudes do change, but "only the truth survives forever." With the mention of truth (*le vrai*), Crébillon's doctrine of the novel enters into complete agreement with the classical exigencies imposed by Boileau: the true, the moral, and the beautiful (*le vrai, le bien et le beau*).[7] For Crébillon, the only solution possible for improvement of the genre was classical limitation, although he was aware that a good number of readers would not tolerate the scourging of adventures, harems, pirates, supernatural encounters and the like. His major novel provided a practical example of reform: in *Les Egarements,* there are no duels, robberies or resurrections; in the leisure society of Meilcour and Mme de Lursay, external wars have ended, and only verbal combat among parlor guests remains. These recommendations parallel the trends of the French classical drama with striking proximity. Crébillon readily admits that excessive simplicity can pose a problem of maintaining interest (see sixth paragraph of Preface). The other alternative had been tried numerous times, however, and had failed.

In the remaining paragraphs of the Preface, readers are advised against the identification of characters in the novel with actual living persons—advice which was necessary in Crébillon's situation, in view of the difficulties encountered with his other publications. One item of interest is found in the next to last paragraph of this important document. The description of Meilcour in these lines and an almost point-by-point summary of *Les Egarements du coeur et de l'esprit* are also innovative in 1736. The other option would be to keep the reader in an arbitrary and uneasy suspense, which was typically the case. Yet Crébillon was willing to go to great length in revealing his story's substance. The subtitle of the novel is the *Mémoires de Monsieur de Meil-*

cour, and the point of view is that of the hero in his upper years, narrating his life in retrospect. The character traits mentioned, "at first simple and unrefined," "ignorance" and "filled with false ideas" serve to emphasize the knowledge and expertise acquired at the end of Meilcour's sentimental education.

Thus Crébillon *fils* provides the French novel of his time with positive "rules" to follow and with a working model to be used in reforming the genre. It is apparent that he was not unique in this endeavor. Nor was he exempt from negative contemporary practices, i.e., criticism of the genre within the genre, so as to separate the new *romans* from the old. When Meilcour experiences his *coup de foudre* upon seeing Mlle de Théville for the first time, he describes his passion as "one of those jolts of surprise which are typical of grand adventures in novels." He would need to call on his familiarity with novels again in making contact with his beloved: "I then recalled all the occasions I had read in novels about how a person should speak to his mistress." In addition, Versac accuses Meilcour of using a "jargon for novels" in his confused attempt to discuss his emotional state.

These denunciations of the genre serve to show that Crébillon *fils* did not consider his work as a *novel* in the commonly accepted meaning of the word. The term as well as the form of the genre would progress toward an acceptable form of art with the passing of time. The publication of *Les Egarements du coeur et de l'esprit* and its Preface in 1736 occured at a propitious moment. Before this date, the French term *roman* was almost always synonymous with insipid romances, and nearly always pejorative; Crébillon undertook to change this association, by allowing for the possibility that the novel could be the most effective literary genre. To accomplish this, however, the theoretician of the novel needed to reach back into the past and take support from an existing model of respect—the comedy. His replacement of the old values of "adventures, intrigues and surprising tricks" by the new values of nature, reason and candor was proof of his foresight. Coincidentally, other authors, Laclos above all, would seek to reinforce the novel by association with classical genres as late as 1784.

NOTES

[1]Crébillon *fils, Les Lettres de la Marquise de M*** au comte de R**** in *OEuvres complètes* (London: n.p., 1779), vol. II. My translation.

[2]Some examples: Lenglet-Dufresnoy, *De l'Usage des romans* (1734); *La Bibliothèque française* (1735); B. Lamy, *La Rhétorique, ou l'Art de parler* (1737); also, Henry Fielding, in *Tom Jones* and *Joseph Andrews.*

[3]My translations of the Preface to *Les Egarements du coeur et de l'esprit* and other portions of that work are based on the edition prepared by Etiemble in vol. II of *Romanciers du XVIIIe siècle* (Paris: Gallimard, 1965).

[4]Etiemble's introduction to the Colin edition of *Les Egarements du coeur et de l'esprit* (Paris: 1961), pp. xxii-xxvii.

[5]Quoted by Emile Henriot in *Les Livres du second rayon* (Paris: Chamontin, 1920), p. 201. The translation and the italics are mine.

[6]On p. 54 of the Gallimard edition, Meilcour becomes so frustrated by Mlle de Théville's indifference toward him that he wished her to trip or even sprain her ankle; thus there is a strong possibility that Crébillon was parodying Marivaux's *Marianne,* who entered public life by means of the same mishap. See also the preceding chapter on Marivaux.

[7]See Boileau's *Préface de 1701* to *l'Art poétique.*

CREBILLON *FILS*: APPENDIX
PREFACE TO
LES EGAREMENTS DU COEUR ET DE L'ESPRIT (1736)

For the most part, Prefaces seem to have been instituted for no other reason than to burden the reader. I disdain this custom too much to follow it. My sole purpose in this one is to announce the goal of these memoirs, so that they be considered either as a purely invented work, or that the adventures which they contain be considered authentic.

The man who writes can have but two aims: the useful and the agreeable. Few authors have succeeded in combining both. He who instructs either disdains entertainment, or has not the talent for it; and the one who entertains does not have enough force to instruct; consequently, the one is always stuffy, and the other is always frivolous.

The novel, so despised by sensible people, and often rightly so, would perhaps be the genre which could be rendered the most useful, if it were well managed, if, instead of filling it with somber and far-fetched stories, with heroes whose characters and adventures always surpass the limit of credibility, if it were made, like comedy, the tableau of human life, and if vice and excess were censured in it.

In truth, the reader would no longer find in it those extraordinary and tragic events which carry away the imagination and which tear the heart in two; no more heroes who cross the seas only to be captured at a given point by Turks; no more intrigues in the harem, no more Sultanas stolen away from the watchful eye of the eunuchs by some surprising trick; no more unexpected deaths; and far fewer subterranean adventures. If the event were prepared with art, it would then be achieved naturally. Reason and proprieties would no longer be violated. Feelings would not be outraged; man would at last see man such as he is; he would be less dazzled, but he would also be more informed.

I confess that many readers who are not moved by simple things, will not tolerate that the novel be stripped of the ostentatious puerilities which have made it dear to them; but in my mind this is not a reason to avoid its reform. Each century, in fact each year inaugurates new tastes. We see authors who write only to be fashionable, and who, victims of their weak obsequiousness, disappear along with it into eternal oblivion. Only the truth survives forever, and if the rabble clamors against it, or has clouded it sometimes, they have never succeeded in destroying it. Any author inhibited by the lowly fear of not pleasing his contemporaries enough, rarely passes on to posterity.

It is true that these novels, which have as their purpose the portrayal of men as they are, are subject to certain problems, aside from their profound simplicity. There are refined readers who never read except to imagine applications, who admire a book only to the degree that they find a way of dishonoring someone, and who apply everywhere in it their malice and bitterness. Could it not be then that these glib people, whose cunning penetrates everywhere, no matter how well concealed, (that these people) would fear, in all probability, that the excess which they noticed in others be attributed to themselves, if they did not hasten to impute it to someone else. From this, however, comes the accusation of an author of having unleashed his wrath against people whom he respects or does not know, and he appears dangerous, although it is his readers alone who are indeed dangerous.

Be that as it may, I know of nothing which should or which can prevent an author from extracting his characters and his portraits from the depths of nature. Specific applications last for only one era; either one tires of them, or they are so superfluous that they eradicate themselves. Moreover, could not the material for these general accounts be found everywhere? The wildest of fictions and the wisest of moral treatises often provide them; and till now, the only works which I know to be exempt from this are books which treat the abstract sciences.

If fops and prudes are to be portrayed, they should not be Mister or Madam such and such, who would have been thought of, but never actually seen; but it seems quite simple to me that if some of them are fops and others prudes, there would be some things which apply to them in those portraits; certainly they would be failures as portraits, if they resembled no one; but it does not ensue, from the mania which some people have in their quest for the identification of others, that one can be depraved or ridiculous with limitless impunity. Ordinarily, one is so un-sure of the identity of characters who have been revealed, that if, in one area of Paris, you heard the shout: "Ah! that must be the Marquess!" you would hear in another area: "I had no idea that the Countess could have been captured so well!", it also hap-pens that even a third person would have been identified at the Court, an assumption which would be no more accurate than the first two.

I have dwelled on this point because, this book being nothing more than a story of private life, of failures and reversals of fortune of a man of quality, one might be more tempted to attribute to persons still living the portraits and adventures con-tained in it, which can be done quite easily; our customs may be depicted in it; Paris may be the scene of its events, but people are not forced to wander off to imaginary regions, and nothing is disguised under primitive names and practices. Concerning the favorable characterizations found in it, I have nothing to add: a virtuous woman, a prudent man—these appear to me as sensible figures who never resemble anyone in particular.

In these memoirs, there will be found a man such as all men are in early youth, at first simple and unrefined, and still un-familiar with the world in which he is forced to live. Parts One and Two revolve around this ignorance and his first love affairs. In the following parts, he is a man filled with wrong ideas and full of ridicule, and who is controlled less by himself than by people interested in corrupting his heart and mind. Finally, in the latter parts, he will be seen as having returned to his senses, and owing all of his good qualities to a respectable woman; therein lies the purpose of the *Wanderings of the Heart and the Mind.* Far be it from my intention to claim that he is presented in all of the disorders which result from passion; love alone pre-vails here; but if another motive is introduced from time to time, it is almost always love which determines him.

No promises or guarantees are made here as to the distribu-tion of this work; the public has been disappointed so many times, that people would be right in not believing the word of the author or publisher; the public can nonetheless rest assured, that if this first Part is found agreeable, all of the other parts will follow in prompt succession.

VI
ROUSSEAU AND THE PERSONAL NOVEL

The central problem in a discussion of Jean-Jacques Rousseau's role as a critic of the novel is one of good faith. This great philosopher and misanthropist presents a fundamental contradiction in that he detested or at least denounced all literature in his *Lettre à D'Alembert sur les spectacles* and elsewhere. At the same time of the publication of *La Nouvelle Héloïse,* one of the greatest successes in fiction in the eighteenth century, there also appeared *L'Emile,* another brilliant success. Yet how ironic that there was room in Emile's curriculum for only one novel, *Robinson Crusoe.* Rousseau himself had read many novels, and wrote a best-seller; his attempts to reconcile his literary activities with his educational theories result in the paradoxical and the arbitrary.

As opposed to the novelists previously considered, Rousseau's case is unique in that he wrote an autobiography after his novel, and thus provided a rare account of the inspiration and creation of *La Nouvelle Héloïse.* Such an account would normally answer innumerable questions on the author's theory and practice of his craft. Yet the credibility of Rousseau's *Confessions* is questionable, because of his many inaccuracies and his acute persecution complex. He furthermore wove this troubled existence into his novel. Rousseau's life was so disappointing that he feared dying without every having lived, and thus utilized fiction as a means of projecting a less troubled, idealized life.

In spite of the above reservations concerning *Les Confessions,* Rousseau's autobiography remains a point of reference for his ideas on the novel. Shortly after the very ambitious preamble of *Les Confessions,* Rousseau reveals himself as an extremely precocious but impressionable youth; his initiation to fiction began almost as soon as he was able to read:

> I know not what I did until five or six years of age; I do
> not know how I learned to read; I remember only my first
> readings and their effect on me: it was the time from
> which I date without interruption the awareness of my-
> self. My mother had left behind some novels. We began
> reading them after dinner, my father and I. At first it
> was a mere question of becoming accustomed to reading
> through amusing books; but soon the interest became so
> vivid, that we both read incessantly, and spent all our
> nights at it. In a short time I gained, by this dangerous
> method, not only an acute reading and comprehension
> skill, but a unique insight into passions for a child my
> age.[1]

In retrospect, the author is able to make some very provoking
comments. His acute self-awareness dates from his initiation to
literature, and later he judged that an innocent reading exercise
had the gravest of consequences on his entire life. His mother's
legacy was composed mainly of novels; their reading was a
"dangerous method," and amounted to a veritable obsession for
Rosseau, and seemingly for his father. The pernicious nature of
fiction is further underscored by a later remark concerning his
mother's library: "Fortunately there were some good books
among them," meaning some Bossuet, Plutarch, Ovid, La
Bruyère, and even some Molière. Novels were apparently not
good books.

Fiction provided Rousseau with a very premature and
dangerous insight into the world of passion. As is seen in the
first preface to *La Nouvelle Héloïse*, he deplored the habit of
allowing children, especially girls, to read novels, a tenet which is
perhaps based on his own disastrous experiences. In Book II of
Les Confessions, he attributed his incapability to cope with
society to the same sources:

> You will laugh when you see me pass myself off as a
> prodigy. Laugh if you will, but when you have finished,
> you will find a child of six for whom novels attract,
> interest, and enrapture to the point of weeping bitterly;
> then shall I feel my absurd vanity, and then shall I admit
> that I am wrong (*Conf.*, p. 61).

Rousseau again indicates his extreme sensitivity to fiction. Although novels were surely not the only source of his difficulties,

he reacted to them in the same manner as he wished the reader of *La Nouvelle Héloïse* to react. We readily imagine Rousseau as a dreamer and an introverted phantast. In subsequent passages of his *Confessions,* he identified his readings in fiction. His favorite novel was D'Urfé's *Astrée:* ". . .among the novels I had read with my father, *L'Astrée* had not been forgotten, and it was the one which came back to my thoughts most often." Rousseau again emphasized the exclusive place occupied by *l'Astrée* in his heart in a letter to Mirabeau dated 22 August 1767.[2]

The modern reader may well wonder why *l'Astrée* was so dear to Rousseau. In truth, D'Urfé's novel was a perfect selection for this "âme romanesque."[3]   The completely artificial setting of shepherds and shepherdesses is as remote as possible from the ugliness of Rousseau's real world. In the pastoral milieu, no mention is made of the mundane details of physical love. The dialogues of Astrée and Céladon are as sublimated as those of Julie and Saint-Preux. In short, *l'Astrée* was for Rousseau an escape into idealized life, as was his own *Nouvelle Héloïse.*

As he grew older, Rousseau frequently came back to his impressionable reading of novels and their importance on his personality:

> I had read every novel; they made me shed buckets of
> tears, even before the age when one becomes attached to
> novels. From this there was born in my heart a heroic
> and adventurous flair which only increased up to the
> present, and which succeeded in making me dislike every-
> thing but that which resembled my caprices.[4]

When Rousseau stated that he had read all novels, his statement warrants some clarification. He had read most of the masterpieces by his contemporaries and immediate predecessors. These included *Gil Blas* (*Conf.,* Livre IV, p. 167), and Duclos' *Confessions du Comte de ***,* a work which caused him to desire a friendship with its author. Duclos eventually became a reader for the early drafts of *La Nouvelle Héloïse* (*Conf.,* Livre VII, p. 284). Rousseau had also read the novels of Prévost, whom he qualified as a ". . .very simple and likeable man whose heart enlivened his writings, which are worthy of immortality, and who had nothing internally nor externally which resembled the somber taint of his works" (*Conf.*, Livre VIII, p. 366). This judgment deserves a comment, since Rousseau was to condemn the excessive sublimity and elevation of spirits found in writers like Prévost and Richardson in the *Entretien sur les romans.* He had read Marivaux's *La Vie de Marianne,* at least Parts I and II, since he ordered the following parts (*C. G.,* I, 54), and *Les Lettres persanes* (*Ibid.,* VII, 271), which he recommended to a friend as a model of style. As for Richardson, he expressed a distinct preference for the novels by the English author, although his remark was relegated to the importance of a footnote in the *Lettre à D'Alembert sur les spectacles* in 1758: "There has never been written, in any language, a novel equal to *Clarissa,* nor even close to it."

Rousseau's role in the history of the eighteenth-century French novel is then unique, since his autobiography and correspondence provide us with accounts of the major novels prior to 1750, without the confusion of terms involved with *roman, roman romanesque, histoire, mémoires,* and so on, as was the case earlier. If Rousseau's readings were up to date, his own concept of *le roman* was not so progressive, but more similar to that shared by other novelists and critics. The first sentence of the Preface to *La Nouvelle Héloïse,* "Theaters are necessary in large cities, and novels are necessary for corrupt people," is as categorical and as striking as the preamble to *Les Confessions.* When Rousseau distributes a parsimonious amount of praise to Prévost and Richardson, his overall concept of literature, the novel included, must be kept in mind. In the polemics following the first *Discours,* he questioned: "How is it that the sciences. . .engender . . .so many ineptitudes, so many bitter satires, so many vile novels, so many licentious poems, so many obscene books?"[5] And within the text of his novel, Rousseau, like so many of his predecessors, did not fail to make passing insults at the genre he practised: in Letter 13 of Part I, Julie warned her preceptor that "to want to move one's mistress by means of novels is to be very little resourceful."[6]

According to Rousseau then, his readings in fiction were too ample for his underdeveloped personality. He took fiction too seriously, and sought to live fiction in his own life. Such were the conditions which surrounded the creation of *La Nouvelle Héloïse.*

Rousseau's fantasies did not close with the projections of himself into fiction: he also intervened extensively in his own novel. "I identified, to the ultimate degree possible, with the lover and friend, attributing to him moreover the virtues and weaknesses which I felt inside myself" (*Conf.*, Livre IX, p. 422). In fact, Rousseau intervenes personally in almost every work of his, as if he could write on nothing but himself. Besides *Les Confessions*, the very model of personal literature, *L'Emile* is not only a treatise on education, but a program of instruction that the author would have liked to receive. Even something which appears so detached and philosophical as the *Lettre à D'Alembert* was provoked by personal attachment to the city of Geneva.

In Books IV and IX of *Les Confessions*, Rousseau explains his selection of the birthplace of Mme de Warens as the site for his novel. His personal life is more visible in Parts III and IV of the novel, which represent the period of his unfulfilled love affair with Sophie D'Houdetot. During this same period, Rousseau's letters abound in notes to and from her, with all of the expected anxieties, sufferings, and rejections. In *Les Confessions*, he claimed that one innocent kiss was the pivotal point in the author's life between happiness and sorrow (*Conf.*, Livre IX, p. 437). This incident is quite similar to the scene of the fatal kiss in Letter 14 of Part I of *La Nouvelle Héloïse*. The sad truth is that Sophie was unable to satisfy Rousseau's complex needs; yet another attractive solution remained, that of imagining an idyllic coexistence by means of fiction.

While it is speculative to say that Saint-Preux was Rousseau, and that Julie was Sophie D'Houdetot, since it is only logical to grant the same literary autonomy to this novel as to any other, the personal involvement of Rousseau in his novel is nonetheless intriguing. The accounts in *Les Confessions* during the 1756-57 period show that the novel had become an obsession for the author:

> I was no longer in control of myself; th∂ delirium per-
> sisted. After many futile efforts to suppress these fanta-
> sies, I was in the end completely seduced by them, and I
> worked at nothing else than to put some order and logic
> in them, to create a sort of novel from them (Livre IX,
> p. 423).

Here in Book IX of *Les Confessions,* Rousseau had not yet reached the periods of frenzy and persecution complexes which were to follow in his later years. The passage does, however, convey the image of a man beset by chaotic, personal obsessions.

In the same passage from *Les Confessions,* the author described even further his chaotic method of composition:

> I scribbled down a few scattered letters, without continuity, without any connection. What is scarcely believable and quite true is that the first two parts were written almost entirely in this manner, without having any organized outline, and without foreseeing that one day I would be inclined to make it an organized work (Livre IX, p. 423).

Although the first letters were more organized than Rousseau would have us believe here, the final four parts of the novel did in fact receive more editorial attention. The decreasing number of letters in the six successive parts bears the proof: the first and longest part contains sixty-five letters; Part II, twenty-eight; Part III, twenty-six; Part IV, seventeen; Part V, fourteen, and the final Part, a mere thirteen letters. The length of each letter does not decrease; in fact, there is an overall increase in the length of individual letters. Rousseau may have attempted to correct his disorganized method of writing Parts I and II.

Rousseau needed fiction as a means of achieving what he could not achieve in real life; his relationship with Mme de Warens was riddled with feelings of incest; Thérèse Levasseur fulfilled only domestic and physical needs; and with Sophie D'Houdetot, he was subordinated to the rank of an unwanted third party. The novel, which was fanciful by definition, was a practical means of keeping open his search for happiness.

Rousseau profited from contemporary trends and practices in prose fiction: he used the epistolary convention, which the public had craved since *Clarissa,* and the memoir novel. He then combined these two aspects into his own *Julie.* The result was a new brand of the memoir novel: new because with Marivaux, Prévost and others, the device of authenticity was readily identifiable as false; but when Rousseau claims to have projected himself into his novel, and when he accounts for this projection in his memoirs, then the line of demarcation between biographical fact (*Les Confessions*) and inspired or created fiction (*La Nouvelle Héloïse*) is no longer as clear.

The second preface to *Julie,* or the *Entretien sur les romans* (see Appendix II), was written in 1759, and published separately several days after the novel. Like most prefatory materials and like his own *Confessions,* the *Entretien* is Rousseau's attempt to justify his novel in the eyes of the public. He states in his first Preface (Appendix I) that he wanted to permit the novel to make its effect on the public before imposing his own views on the issue. Similar to other prefacers, he hoped that "some useful ideas will be found in it as to the purpose of novels." The *Entretien* is further important because it contains Rousseau's most lengthy development of his ideas on the novel; it poses numerous problems, and the solutions are often insufficient, if not contradictory.

The *Entretien* takes the form of a conversation between Rousseau (R.), still clinging to his role of *éditeur,* and N., who appears at times as an average reader, at other times like one of the *philosophes,* or even as a royal censor. Rousseau describes him as follows:

> It contains the sentiments of a man of letters and of good taste to whom I claim to have lent my manuscript, and in whose place I tried to put myself in order to judge it as critically as he would have judged it. While criticizing myself, I did not relinquish the right to defend myself, and so that neither the interest of truth nor of editorship be forgotten, I executed as faithfully as possible the ideas of the censor and my own in the form of a dialogue (*C. G.,* 45-46).

N.'s severity is somewhat of an exaggeration. His objections are merely a framework for the *pro domo* defense of *La Nouvelle Héloïse.*

One of the major reasons for the success of *La Nouvelle Héloïse* was that many readers thought that it was a real story; it actually began a search for the real site of Wolmar's estate and the real characters by its readers, and Rousseau attempted to exploit this success to the fullest. When N. laments on page xii,

"Oh! if she had really existed," and again at the end of the dialogue, ". . .but say that these two women have really existed, and I will read their epistles once a year to the end of my life" (xxxv), he is paying homage to the author, since this is precisely the desired effect. It costs Rousseau nothing to say that the question of fact versus fiction is inconsequential, having already won the argument.

In view of N.'s persistence, however, he is forced into a discussion of more serious esthetic questions. If the reader is to consider *La Nouvelle Héloïse* as purely fictional, then N. argues that the genre can admit all the exaggerations imaginable: monsters, giants, dwarfs, chimeras (xii). For N. and for the advocates of realism, the characters of Rousseau's novel are too good to be true. Julie's conversion after her sin, Wolmar's acceptance of his wife's former lover in his home, and similar incidents are too ideal to be believed, especially when contrasted with the narration of domestic banalities in the novel. R. reminds N. of the required perspective, that of reading a collection of letters—not a novel—and the only acceptable perspective for Rousseau.

Rousseau's general opinion of *les romans* was by no means favorable, and except for a few peculiar preferences, he meant by the term *roman romanesque* or romance, i.e., lengthy adventure tales. Like any respectable author, he obviously sought to avoid being grouped with authors such as La Calprenède.[7] As for the plot of his novel, he singled it out from all other works of the same genre, because of its *simplicity:*

> What was noticed the least, and will always make it a
> unique work, is the simplicity of the subject matter and
> the chain of interest which, centered on three people, is
> maintained throughout six volumes, without digression,
> without exaggerated adventure, without mischievousness
> of any kind, neither in the characters, nor in their actions
> (*Conf.,* Livre XI, p. 537).

In the same passage, Rousseau compared Part IV of *La Nouvelle Héloïse* to *La Princesse de Clèves,* the classical masterpiece of simplicity in prose fiction.

When N. points out in the "Dialogue" that R.'s need for variety could justify the presence of monsters and giants in the novel, R. could defend himself. He does center his novel on three characters for the most part. Whether *La Nouvelle Héloïse* is in fact written "without digression, without exaggerated adventure, without mischievousness of any kind, neither in the characters nor in their actions," is a different matter. *La Nouvelle Héloïse* is not difficult to read because of its plot line, but because of its filler material, letters of thirty pages or more in length, which give it the appearance of a philosophical tract. The major digressions are the treatise on duels (I, 57); on Paris, (II, 13-17); marriage and adultery, (III, 18); suicide, (III, 21-22); atheism, (V, 5); Geneva, (VI, 5); and prayer and liberty, (VI, 6-8). These digressive letters are in part justified by the fact that they were current social and philosophical issues in Rousseau's mind in 1761. They are from the pen of the philosopher rather than the lyric novelist. The most striking example of Rousseau's oratorical zeal is found in the second and third letters of Part V, where Saint-Preux describes life at Wolmar's estate for more than sixty pages (in the Gallimard edition). The editor's explanation, that the letters of a recluse are few and far between, and therefore can tend to be rather long, seems equivocal. Once again, Rousseau was bogged down in the antithetical motives of writing a simple novel, and imposing his personal views of human existence at the same time.

After comparing Part IV of *La Nouvelle Héloïse* to the classical and dramatic simplicity of *La Princesse de Clèves,* Rousseau undertook to reconcile his work with another landmark in the genre, Samuel Richardson. The comparison of his novel with those of the English genius was in part provoked by Rousseau's ever-deteriorating relationship with Diderot, and ultimately with the latter's *Eloge de Richardson,* which appeared at the same time that Rousseau wrote the eleventh book of his *Confessions.* In fact, he had communicated his manuscript of the novel to Diderot for advice in late 1756:

> Nearly six months had passed since I sent to him the first two parts of *Julie,* so that he could give me his opinion of it. He still had not read them. We read one notebook of it together. He found it all padded ["feuil-lu"], that was his term; that is, packed with words and redundant. I had felt the same thing myself; but it was due to the ramblings of my passion; I was never able to correct it. The last parts are not like that. The fourth,

especially, and the sixth, are masterpieces of expression
(*Conf.*, Livre IX, pp. 451-52).

Diderot had pinpointed objections that would strike the average
reader, and that N. was to bring out in the *Entretien.* We have
already witnessed Rousseau's feverish disposition at the moment
of composing Parts I and II; but five years later, the author was
not as willing to admit these stylistic weaknesses. Whereas
Diderot praised the great variety found in Richardson's novels,
Rousseau countered with his control of the number of characters:

> Richardson has, in effect, the distinction of characterizing
> them all quite well: but, as for their number, he is similar
> to the most insipid novelists, who reinforce the sterility
> of their ideas by virtue of characters and intrigues. It is
> easy to arouse attention by presenting incessantly un-
> heard-of events and new faces which pass by like the
> figures of a magic lantern; but to maintain one's interest
> with the same subjects, without miraculous adventures,
> that is certainly more difficult; and if, all things being
> equal, the simplicity of the subject adds to the beauty of
> the work, Richardson's novels, which are superior in so
> many other aspects, would not be able to enter on the
> same level as mine on this point (*Conf.*, Livre XI, pp.
> 537-38).

Rousseau is again contradictory: the difference made by the
three years from the *Lettre à D'Alembert,* where he categorically
stated that Richardson's novels were unsurpassed from all points
of view, is considerable. Here is Book XI of *Les Confessions,* the
author of *Clarissa* is grouped with authors of insipid *romans
romanesques* of the preceding centuries. Surely the verbiage in
Clarissa is more pertinent to the actions of the heroine and
Richard Lovelace than are the letter-digressions in *La Nouvelle
Héloïse.* The sole means of reconciling this reversal of opinion
is to consider the circumstances in which it was written. By the
time of the above-quoted condemnation (1770), Rousseau had
already broken with Diderot, Grimm, and the other *philosophes,*
and his criticism of Richardson is not to be considered as such,
but more as a riposte to the *Eloge de Richardson,* and more precisely, to its author.

The central technical problem of *La Nouvelle Héloïse* was Rousseau's choice of narrative mode. Richardson had established the epistolary vogue with his best-seller, *Clarissa Harlowe*. Rousseau, in a moment of humility, admitted his own shortcomings in the letter genre: ". . .as with letters, a genre whose tone I was never able to seize, and whose practice is torture for me" (*Conf.*, Livre III, 112). On two other occasions, Rousseau criticized his own letter style, in the beginning of Part II of the novel, where he apologized for the disorder and bad style of the two lovers, and secondly in Letter 16 of Part II, where Saint-Preux thanks Julie for her criticism of his absurd letters. Finally, when N. cries out in the *Entretien:* "What an epistolary style! How full of bombast! What exclamations! What preparation! How emphatical to express common ideas!" (p. xiv), R.'s defense of his weak style is long and questionable, but worth noting. According to R., the style of *La Nouvelle Héloïse* is unique, and for very good reasons. In society, people tend to speak as others would want them to speak, in order to compete and to convince, whereas with isolated, rural people, the style is less refined, and consequently less hypocritical:

> On the contrary, a letter really dictated by love and written by a lover influenced by a real passion, will be tame, diffuse, prolix, unconnected, and full of repetitions; his heart overflowing with the same sentiment, constantly returns to the same expressions, and, like a natural fountain, flows continually without being exhausted (xvi).

The author-editor of *La Nouvelle Héloïse* is saying in effect that the awkward style of a letter is proof of its authenticity. Whether or not Saint-Preux's monotonous letters and spontaneous style are justified by his passionate state of mind is speculative; yet Rousseau's reader may find it somewhat difficult to believe that passion could have dictated Saint-Preux's two consecutive letters of thirty pages in length in Part IV.

As one might expect from his other writings, Rousseau was a moralist in matters regarding the novel. The *Lettre à D'Alembert* shows that his opinion of the moral capabilities of literature was extremely low. Also, in Book III of *L'Emile*, the philosopher of education stated peremptorily that he detested books.[8] His pupil was allowed to read no other novel that *Robinson Crusoe* because it was a novel "stripped of all its rubbish,"[9] and because of obvious analogies with the personal life of Jean-Jacques Rousseau. When Saint-Preux suggested discarding most books as part of a reformed curriculum for Julie in Letter 12 of Part I, it was more the author of *L'Emile* speaking than the "éditeur" of these letters. In Letter 21 of Part II, Rousseau had to make another exception as he had to for *Robinson Crusoe:*

> Novels are perhaps the last form of instruction which remains to be given to a nation which is so corrupt that all other means become useless; I would then prefer that the composition of this sort of books be allowed only by righteous but sensitive persons, whose feelings are depicted in their writings, by authors who are not above human weaknesses, who do not describe virtue as being beyond man's reach, and yet who make one love it by describing it as being less severe at first, and that later, they would subtly lead men to it from the midst of vice.

If Rousseau had to constantly modify his precepts, it might have been due to the fact that, as he points out in the *Entretien,* no one listened to him when he tried to address men. He was misunderstood both during his life and in recent times. The paradox of the man who denounced novels while writing one could be resolved by the fact that novels were more effective for those who lived apart from society, another idea expressed in the *Entretien sur les romans.*

Rousseau's long argument for exhorting people to do good in the "Dialogue" is summarized in the following pasage from *Les Confessions,* Livre IX, pp. 426-27:

> Surely the greatest advantage to be taken from my follies was the love for goodness, which I never lost sight of for a moment, which turned them toward useful goals, and whose moral lesson was allowed to make its full impression. Perfect creatures do not exist in nature, and their lessons are not close enough to us. But when a young woman who is born with a heart as tender as it is honest, is vanquished by love as a girl, and discovers enough strength to conquer it in turn as an adult, when she regains virtue, whoever might say to you that this entire tableau is scandalous and useless is a liar and a hypocrite; do not listen to him.

Rousseau was confident of having accomplished what no one else could accomplish, teaching morality in a genre where all others had failed. He created a hell on earth for his characters, followed by a heaven on earth which, in spite of Julie's confession of undying love for Saint-Preux at the end of the novel, sufficed to the task.

There remains to account for the central paradox of Rousseau's literary career, that of the self-avowed hater of literature who wrote something as odious as a novel. According to the Rousseau who wrote the preface to *Narcisse* in 1752, there was no contradiction; it was merely necessary to condescend to the level of man's corruption by literature, in order to deter him from greater evils:

> I now ask where lies the contradiction of practising myself certain tastes of which I approve the progress? It is no longer a question of motivating people to do good; all one can do is distract them from doing evil; they must be occupied with trivialities in order to be distracted from immoral acts. If my writings have edified the small number of good people, I performed all of the goodness which depended on me, and perhaps it is an even more useful service when they are offered other objects of entertainment which prevent them from thinking about them.[10]

This is still the Rousseau of the *Discours* and the *Lettre à D'Alembert.* Almost twenty years later, however, Rousseau confronted the problem of his hypocrisy more seriously, in a moment of sobriety in the *Confessions:*

> My major embarrassment was the shame of contradicting myself so blatantly and so publicly. After the austere principles which I had just established with so much ado, after the severe maxims I had preached widely, after so many stinging invectives against effeminate books which exude love and weakness, could one image anything more unexpected, more shocking than to see me all of a sudden write my name among authors of these books which I had censured so harshly. I felt this inconsistency in its full force, I reproached myself for it, I blushed at it, I disappointed myself because of it: but the entire matter was

inadequate to return me to my senses. Completely overwhelmed, I had to submit myself at any cost, and resign
myself to withstand the public's criticism, with the exception of later deliberation as to whether I would have my
book shown or not (*Conf.*, Livre IX, 426).

This is Jean-Jacques Rousseau the novelist "dans toute la vérité
de la nature," an author condemned to a set of principles that he
had fabricated for himself, and from which there was no escape.
The preceding admission of hypocrisy shows the degree to which
the rules of the *Entretien sur les romans* are to be taken seriously, as well as the denunciations of the novel in the preface to the
most successful French novel of the eighteenth century.

NOTES

[1]My translations of Rousseau's *Confessions,* as well as the page references, are based on the edition prepared by Louis Martin-Chauffier (Paris: Gallimard, 1933). The quoted passage is from Livre I, p. 8. Subsequent references to this work are abbreviated by *Conf.*

[2]Rousseau, *Correspondance générale,* ed. by T. Dufour and Pierre-Paul Plan (Paris: Plon, 1924-34), XVII, 220. All references to Rousseau's correspondence are based on this edition, referred to hereafter as *C. G.*

[3]The qualification is that of Jean-Louis Lecercle, in *Rousseau et l'art du roman* (Paris: Colin, 1969), chapter 1.

[4]Letter to Malesherbes, dated Jan. 12, 1762, in *C. G.,* VII, 49.

[5]Quoted by Lecercle, p. 33.

[6]Rousseau, *Julie, ou La Nouvelle Héloïse, in OEuvres complètes de Rousseau,* ed. by Bernard Gagnebin and Marcel Raymond (Paris: Gallimard, 1961), II, 62. My translations of the novel and of the two Prefaces are based on this critical edition.

[7]In Book IV of *L'Emile,* Rousseau presents La Calprenède, and more specifically his *Cléopâtre* and *Cassandre* as examples of distortions of historical truth, and concludes with "I see little difference between these novels and your histories. . ."

[8]Rousseau, *Emile* (Paris: Garnier, 1961), 210.

[9]*Ibid.,* 211.

[10]Rousseau, *OEuvres complètes,* II, 972.

ROUSSEAU: APPENDIX I
PREFACE TO
LA NOUVELLE HELOISE (1761)

Theaters are necessary in large cities, and novels are necessary for corrupt people. I have witnessed the morals of my time, and I have published these letters. If only I could have lived in an age when I should have thrown them in the fire!

Although I am limited to the role of mere editor here, I have contributed to this work, and I make no attempt to conceal it. Did I write the entire work, and is the whole correspondence fictitious? People of the world, what difference does it make to you? For you, it will certainly be fiction.

Every honest man ought to acknowledge the books which he published. I, therefore, name myself at the beginning of this collection, not to attribute it to me, but to be able to account for it. If there are weaknesses, let them be my fault; if there are some good elements, I will not seek the praise. If the book is bad, I am all the more obligated to own it; I make no effort to pass myself off as someone better than I really am.

As for the truth in these deeds, since I traveled to the country of the two lovers, I declare that I have never heard of the Baron d'Etange or his daughter, nor of Lord Edouard Bomston, Mr. Orbe or Mr. Wolmar. I must also warn the reader that the script was seriously altered in several places, and whether this was intentional or accidental, I did not know. That is all I am permitted to say. May everyone draw his own conclusions.

This book was not designed for wide circulation, and will suit very few readers. The style will offend people of taste; the content will upset the austere; each sentiment will seem unnatural to those who do not accept virtue. It will probably displease the devout, the lax and the philosophers; it may shock flirtatious women and scandalize modest women. Whom will it please, then? Perhaps only me, but it is certain that it will please no one in a moderate degree.

Whoever resolves to read these letters should arm himself with patience against the grammatical errors, the flat and peremptory style, and the pedantry of the ideas; he will probably say to himself that those who write here are not Frenchmen, wits, academicians or philosophers, but that they are countrymen, foreigners, recluses, young people, almost children, who mistake the romantic fantasies of their minds for philosophy.

Why would I fear to say what is on my mind? This collection of letters with its gothic tone is better suited to women than are philosophical books. It could even be of use to those who, during a corrupted life, preserved some amount of love for honesty. As for girls, that is a different matter. No chaste girl has ever read a novel, and I have placed this one under a sufficiently clear title so that people would know what to expect when they open it. Any girl who, in spite of the title, would dare to read one single page; is lost; but she should not blame this book for her loss, because the harm was done before. Since she has begun, she may as well continue reading; she has nothing more to lose.

If, during the reading of this work, the austere person is shocked by the first sections, casts it down in anger, is indignant at the editor, I shall not complain of his injustice; instead, I could have done the same. But if someone dared to blame me for publishing it after reading it in entirety, let him, if he so pleases, tell it to all the world; but I do not want him to come and tell it to me; I do not feel that I could ever respect such a man.

ROUSSEAU: APPENDIX II
SECOND PREFACE:
ENTRETIEN SUR LES ROMANS (1761)

Foreword

This dialogue or supposed conversation was originally intended to serve as a preface to the Letters of these two lovers; but since its form and length would have permitted me only an abridged version at the beginning of the work, I provide it here in its complete form, in the hope that some useful ideas will be found in it as to the purpose of novels. I initially felt it proper to wait until the book had made its first impressions before discussing its strengths and weaknesses, since I wished no harm to the bookseller, nor did I want to solicit the indulgence of the public.

Dialogue

N.   Here is your manuscript. I have read it completely.

R.   Completely? I take that to mean: you do not expect to have many people imitating you.

N.   *Vel duo, vel nemo.*

R.   *Turpe et miserabile.** But I want to have your frank opinion.

---

*   N.   Either two, or none at all.

R.   Shameful and wretched.

N.   I do not dare.

R.   You have dared everything by that one word. Explain yourself.

N.   My opinion depends on the answer that you are about to give me. Is this correspondence real, or merely fictitious?

R.   I fail to see the point. In order to say that a book is good or bad, what difference does it make to know how it was created?

N.   It makes a great deal of difference in this case. A portrait's value is based on the likeness, however strange the original subject might be. But in a creative picture, every human trait should be common to all men, or else the picture is worthless. Yet supposing that they are both good, one more difference remains: the portrait will be of interest to few people; only the picture can please the public in general.

R.   I follow you. If these letters are portraits, they will be of no interest; if they are pictures, they have a poor likeness. Isn't that it?

N.   Precisely.

R.   Thus I will have drawn out all your answers before you have even spoken. Besides, since I cannot answer your question to your satisfaction, I must ask you one of my own. Let us suppose the worst. My Julie. . .

N.   Oh! if she had really existed!

R.   Well, then?

N.   But surely this is nothing more than a fiction.

R.   If you wish.

N.   In that case, I know of nothing more upsetting. These letters are not letters at all; this novel is not a novel; the characters are inhabitants of the other world.

R.   I am sorry, especially for this world.

N.   Console yourself; there is no lack of fools here, either; but yours are not taken from nature.

R.   I could. . .No, I see the direction that your curiosity is taking. Why do you judge like that? Do you know how widely men differ, how opposite characters are, how much customs and prejudices vary from one era to the next, from place to place, and from age to age? Who would dare to impose precise limits on nature and say: This is the point to which men may go, and no further?

N.   With that type of reasoning, monsters, giants, pygmies and chimeras of all kinds could be specifically admitted into nature; every object would be disfigured, and we would no longer have a common model. I repeat: in paintings depicting humanity, everyone should be able to recognize men.

R.   I agree, on the condition that we also be able to discern the variety in human nature and that which is essential to it. What would you have to say about those who would not recognize our nature unless it were dressed in French clothing?

N.   And what would you have to say about the person who, without expressing features or shape, would want to paint a human figure with a mere veil for clothing? Would we not have the right to ask where the man is?

R.   Neither features nor shape? Is this fair? There is the illusion: There are no perfect people. A young woman who offends the virtue which is dear to her, who is led back to her duty out of fear of an even greater crime; a too easy friend, punished by her own heart for her excessive indulgence; an honest and sensitive young man, filled with weakness and fine words; an old gentleman who prides himself on his nobility and who sacrifices everything to opinion; an Englishman who is generous and brave, constantly and fervently wise, and who reasons without reason. . .

N.   A hospitable and debonnaire husband who hastens to welcome into his home his wife's former lover. . .

R.   I refer you to the inscription on the plate.

N.   *Les belles âmes!* . . . How fine!

R.   Oh philosophy! What pains you take to constrict the heart, and to make men small!

N.   A romantic imagination aggrandizes them and fools them. But let us continue. The two friends—what have you to say about them? And that sudden conversion at the altar? Divine grace, no doubt?

R.   Sir. . .

N.   A pious Christian woman who does not teach her children their catechism, who dies without imploring God, and yet whose death edifies a parson and converts an atheist! Oh!

R.   Sir. . .

N.   As for the interest, it must be universal, or it does not exist. Not one single bad act; not one wicked man to make us fear for the good. Events which are so natural and simple that they are too simple; nothing surprising or dramatic. Everything is quite easily predictable; everything takes place as expected. What is the use of keeping an account of what can be seen every day, at home or at the neighbor's?

R.   So you mean that you need common men and rare deeds? I think I would prefer the opposite. Moreover, you are judging what you have read as a novel. It is not a novel; you said so yourself. It is a collection of letters.

N.   Letters which are not letters. I think I also said that. What an epistolary style! How full of bombast! What exclamations! What preparation! How emphatical to express common ideas! What great words to convey petty reasonings! Rarely is there any sense or accuracy; never any finesse, strength or depth. A diction which is always sublime and thoughts which remain pedestrian. If your characters are to be found in nature, you must confess that their style is hardly natural.

R.   I agree that, from your point of view, things might

seem as they do to you.

N.   Do you think that the public will view it any differently? And is it not my view which you are seeking?

R.   It is in order to have it more developed that I answer you. I now see that you would prefer to have letters written expressedly for publication.

N.   This seems to be the proper opinion for those which are suitable for printing.

R.   Then in books, men will be seen only as they wish to appear?

N.   Rather the author as he wished to appear, and those whom he depicts such as they are. But this advantage is still lacking here. Not one single portrait vigorously painted; not one character clearly delineated; no sound observation; no familiarity with the world. What is there to learn in the tiny sphere of two or three lovers who are always and only concerned with themselves?

R.   You can learn to love humanity. In refined society, you can learn only to hate men.

Your judgment is harsh; the public's ought to be even more so. Without complaining of injustice, I do want to tell you from what angle I view these letters, not so much to excuse the weaknesses which you note, but rather to locate their source.

In a secluded situation, one has different manners of seeing and feeling than in the routine of society; passions which are modified differently have also different expressions; the imagination, which remains concentrated on the same objects, is more vividly affected by them. This small number of images continuously recurs, mixes with our ideas, and gives them this strange and uniform tone which can be noticed in the speech of people who live in solitude. Does it ensue from that that their language is energetic? Not at all; it is simply exceptional. It is only in society that we learn to speak with energy. First of all because we are forced to speak differently and better than others, and, since we must constantly confirm what we do not believe, express feelings we do not have, the result is that we add to what we say a persuasive manner which replaces interior persuasion. Do you believe that truly sensitive people have those vivid, emphatic and ardent manners of speech which you admire in your dramas and novels? No; true passion, full of itself, is expressed more with abundance than with force; it is not interested in persuasion; it never suspects that it might be questioned. When it says what it feels, it is less a matter of its own comfort than of revelation to others. Love is represented with more energy in large cities; but is it felt better there than in the villages?

N.   You mean that weakness of the expression is proof of the strength of the passion?

R.   Sometimes, at least, it is an indication of its existence. Read a love letter written by an author in his study, or by a man of wit who wants to shine. If there is any ardor within him, his letter will set the paper on fire, so it is said; but the heat will not radiate any further. You may be charmed, perhaps even moved; but it will be a fleeting and sterile agitation which will leave you mere words for memories. On the contrary, a letter really dictated by love and written by a lover influenced by a real passion will be tame, diffuse, prolix, unconnected, and full of repetitions; his heart, overflowing with the same sentiment, constantly returns to the same expressions, and like a natural fountain, flows continually without being exhausted. Nothing striking or remarkable; the words, expressions and sentences are all forgotten; we admire nothing in it, we are struck by nothing. And yet, we feel that our souls have been moved, and without knowing why. If we are not struck by the force of the sentiment, we are touched by its truth, and that is how one heart communicates with another. But insensitive people and those who use nothing but the embellished jargon of passions, are familiar with these particular beauties, and they scorn them.

N.   I am still waiting.

R.   All right. In this last form of letters, if the thoughts are ordinary, the style is not and should not be familiar. Love is nothing more than an illusion; it creates, shall we say, another world for itself; it surrounds itself with objects that do not exist, and to which it gives life; since it creates images of all our senti-

ments, its language is always figurative. But those figures are
always imprecise and irregular; its eloquence resides in its disorder; when it reasons the least, it is then that it is the most
convincing. Enthusiasm is the ultimate degree of passion. When
it is most intense, its object appears as being perfect; it then becomes its idol; it is placed in the heavens; and since the enthusiasm of devotion uses the language of love, the enthusiasm of love
uses the same language of devotion. It sees nothing but paradise,
angels, saintly virtues, the delights of heaven. In such a transport, in view of such elevated images, could one talk in vulgar
words? Can one decide to debase and defile those ideas by common expressions? Would one not elevate his style? Would it not
be given grandeur and dignity? How can you talk about letters,
or about letter style? When you write to your beloved, is that
what it is about? You no longer write letters, but hymns.

N.   Citizen, are you feeling well?

R.   No. You see the whiteness upon my head. There is
an age proper to experience, and another for memories. Our
sensitivity disappears with time; but the sensitive soul remains
forever.

I return to the subject of our letters. If you read them as
the work of an author interested in pleasing or who prides himself on his writing, then they are detestable. But take them for
what they are, and judge them in their own kind. Two or three
simple young people, but sensitive people, discuss the interests
of their own hearts. They do not think of impressing the others.
They know and love one another too much for self-interest to
become involved. They are young, but will they think as
adults? They are not French, so can they write correctly? They
are isolated, and will they know the world and its society? Filled
with one unique sentiment, they are feverish, and they think
that they philosophize. Do you expect them to observe, judge
and reflect? They know nothing of those things. They know
how to love, and they relate everything to their love. Is the importance which they give to their follies any less amusing than
all of the wit they could have displayed? They talk about everything; they are mistaken about everything; they inform us of
nothing but themselves; but in revealing themselves, they become
dear to us. Their mistakes are worth more than the wisdom of
prophets. Everywhere, even in error, their honest hearts bear

the mark of virtue, ever confident and ever betrayed. They are heard and answered by nothing, while everything disillusions them. They turn a deaf ear to the voice of discouragement; finding nowhere what they feel, they turn inward and detach themselves from the rest of the world; and they create for themselves a little world different from our own, which presents an entirely new scene.

N. I agree that a twenty year-old man and a girl of eighteen ought not be expected to speak as or consider themselves as philosophers, whatever their education may have been. I must also admit, and this difference has not escaped me, that these girls become women of merit, and the young man a better observer. I make no comparison between the beginning and the end of the work. The details of domestic life erase the youthful mistakes; the chaste wife, the sensible woman, the mother worthy of her family make us forget the sinful lover. But that is precisely a subject of criticism: the end of the collection renders the beginning all the more blameworthy; one could say that they are two different books that the same group of people should not read. In view of the necessity to portray rational characters, why show them before they become rational? The child's play which precedes the lessons of wisdom prevents them from attaining it; we are scandalized by the evil before we can be edified by the goodness; finally, the indignant reader revolts and abandons the work just as he is about to profit from it.

R. I feel, on the contrary, that the end would be superfluous to those who were revolted by the beginning, and that this beginning ought to be agreeable to those who find the end useful. Thus, those who do not complete the work will have lost nothing, since it is not suited to them; and those who can profit from it would not have read it if it had begun on a more severe note. In order to make useful what you wish to convey, you must first have the attention of those whom you wish to use it.

I have changed my means, but not my end. When I tried to address men, no one listened to me; perhaps in addressing children will I fare better; and children are no more inclined to accept the bare truth than an ill-disguised medicine. . .

My people are lovable; but to love them at the age of thirty, they must be seen at the age of twenty. One must have lived a long time with them to be content among them; and it is only after denouncing their mistakes that one succeeds in appreciating their virtues. Their letters are not interesting at first; but little by little they intrigue us; we cannot pick them up or leave them. All charm and ease are absent, as are reason, wit and eloquence; but feeling is there; it is gradually felt in the heart, and it supplants all else in the end. It is a long romance, whose individual parts will not be touching, but which produces an effect as a whole. That is what I experience in reading them; tell me if you feel the same thing.

N. No. Yet I can understand this effect with you. If you are the author, the effect is quite simple; if you are not, I can still understand. A man who dwells in the world cannot be accustomed to the extravagant ideas, affected sympathy, and false reasoning of your fine people. A recluse can appreciate them; you have provided the explanation yourself. But before publishing this manuscript, remember that the public is not composed of hermits. The most fortunate thing that could happen would be that your good young man be taken for a Celadon, your Edouard for a Don Quixote, your damsels for two Astrées, and that everyone will laugh at them as if they were fools. But lengthy follies lose their humor. One must write like Cervantes in order to maintain the reader's interest in six volumes of nonsense.

R. I am encouraged to publish this work for the same reason that you would suppress it.

N. What! The certainty of never being read?

R. Have a bit of patience and you shall hear me out.

When it is a matter of morals, there is no reading which is more useful to people of the world, in my mind. First because the multitude of books which they glance at, and which state the positive and then the negative, mutually destroy the effect of both, and make the entire lot meaningless. Those few books chosen for a second reading are also ineffective; if they are written in support of general opinions, they are extraneous; and if they oppose them, they are equally useless. They are too weak to break the chain which attaches the reader to society's vices. A man of the world may possibly want to conform his behavior to the moral order; but he will encounter such resistance from all sides, that he will be forced to resume his initial position. I am convinced that there are few well-born people who have not attempted this at least once in their lives; but they are soon discouraged by the futility; they abandon it, and content themselves with considering the morality of books as the prattle of loafers. The more one is removed from commerce, from large cities and populous societies, the fewer obstacles there are. There is a point at which these obstacles cease to be invincible, and it is then that books can be of some use. When one lives in isolation, and since reading is not done for ostentation, the readings are less varied, and there is more reflection on them; and since they meet less interference from without, their effect is greater from within. Boredom, that scourge of solitude as well as of society, forces a return to entertaining books, the sole resource of he who lives alone and who finds no entertainment from within himself. Many more novels are read in the provinces than in Paris; more are read in the country than the city, and they are more effective there; you do see why that is.

But these books which could be entertaining, informative, consoling to the retired people who are unfortunate only in their imagination, seem created rather to mock their condition, by increasing the erroneous reason for that mockery. People of grand appearance, fashionable women, the great, the military—those are the actors of all your novels. The refinement of city taste, the rules of the court, the splendor of luxury, and epicurean morality—those are the lessons they preach and the rules that they give. The coloring of their false virtues tarnished the glow of true ones; social manners are substituted for actual duties; fine discourses cause fine actions to be disdained, and the simplicity of virtuous behavior is seen as crudeness.

What effect will such scenes produce on a country lord who sees ridiculed the candor with which he welcomes his guests, and who sees the joy which he brings into his domain treated as a crude form of amusement? What would be the effect on his wife who would discover that the cares of a mother are beneath a woman of her station? Or on her daughter whose affected airs and jargon of the city would cause her to disdain the honest country neighbor whom she would have married?. . .

Authors, men of letters and philosophers are constantly

yelling that to be a good citizen and to serve one's fellow man, we must live in large cities; to flee Paris is, according to them, the equivalent of hatred of the human race; country people are nothing to them; to hear them talk one would say that men can be found only in hotels, academies and open tables.

The same trend is about to occur in all areas. Provincials are being attacked in tales, novels, and dramas. They are jeering at the simplicity of rural life; everything exalts the manners and pleasures of high society: it is shameful not to be familiar with them; it is a disaster not to try them. Who knows by how many common thieves and prostitutes the attraction of these fugitive pleasures populates Paris from one day to the next? Thus, since prejudice and popular opinion reinforce the results of political systems, they heap and pile up inhabitants of every country into some isolated points of the land, leaving all the rest fallow and deserted; thus, in order to make the capital cities glitter, nations depopulate themselves; and this frivolous attraction which catches the eye of the ignorant is causing Europe to rush toward its own destruction. It is important for man's happiness to try to halt this onslaught of poisoned precepts. The work of preachers consists of shouting to us: "Be good and wise," without being too concerned about the success of their speeches; the citizen who is concerned is not required to stupidly shout to us: "Be good", but should make us love the state which causes us to be good.

N. Just one moment: catch your breath. I like useful opinions; and I followed you so attentively in this one that I feel I can preach for you.

It is clear, according to your reasoning, that to give to creative works the only utility that they are capable of, they would have to be directed at a goal contrary to the one proposed by their authors; remove all structured elements; bring everything back to nature; instill in men the love of the regular, simple life; cure them of the caprices of public opinion; give them again the taste for true pleasures; make them love solitude and peace; keep them at some distance from their fellow man; and instead of inciting them to be crammed into the cities, have them spread equally throughout the land, so as to make it prosper in all sections. I understand further that it is not a question of creating Daphnis, Sylvanders, pastors of Arcadia, shepherds of Lignon, illustrious peasants cultivating their lands with their own hands, and speculating on nature, nor any other comparable fictitious beings who can exist nowhere but in books; but it is rather a question of showing well-to-do people that country life and agriculture have pleasures which they do not know how to appreciate; that these pleasures are less insipid, less primitive than they think; that refinement, selection and delicacy can prevail there; that a man of worth who would like to withdraw to the country with his family and become his own farmer could spend just as pleasant a life there as in the midst of the attractions of cities; that a country woman can be a charming one, just as full of grace, and a more touching kind of grace than all of the foppish women; finally, that the most gentle of human feelings can enliven a more pleasant society than the affected language of snobbish gatherings, where our bitter and satirical laughter is the sad result of the happiness which we no longer know. Is that it?

R.   That is precisely it.   To which I will add only one thought. People complain that novels burden their minds; I believe it. While incessantly showing to those who read them the supposed charms of a condition which is not their own, they seduce them, they cause them to hold their condition in contempt, and have them make an imaginary exchange of the one that they are made to love. Wishing to be what they are not, they succeed in believing themselves to be something other than what they are, and there is how one becomes mad. If novels offered to their readers nothing but portrayals of the things which surround them, nothing but the duties which they can do, nothing but the pleasures of their situation, then novels would not drive them mad, they would make them wise. Books written for solitary people must speak their language: to instruct them, they must be pleasing to them, and they must interest them; they must associate them to their state by making it agreeable to them. They must combat and destroy the maxims of great societies; they must prove them to be false and scornful, that is, just as they are. In view of all these aspects a novel, if it is done well, at least if it is of some use, ought to be booed, hated, decried by people in fashion, as a flat, extravagant and absurd book; and there, sir, is how worldly folly becomes wisdom.

N.   Your conclusion is self-evident.   One cannot better foresee one's downfall, nor prepare to fall more proudly. I have one more problem. As you know, provincials read only on our recommendation: they receive only what we send them. A book intended for solitary individuals is judged first by the mundane; if the latter reject it, the others do not read it. Answer that.

R.   The answer is easy. You are talking of the fashionable provincial set; and I am talking about true rural people. You others who shine in the capital city, you have prejudices of which you must be cured; you think you set the tone for all of France, and three quarters of France does not know that you even exist. The books which fail in Paris make a fortune for provincial booksellers.

N.   Why do you wish to make them rich at the expense of our own?

R.   Mock me, but I will persist. When one seeks after glory, one must be read in Paris; when one wants to be useful, one must be read in the provinces. How many decent people spend their lives in isolated regions to cultivate their paternal heritage, where they look on themselves as being exiled by a scant amount of wealth? During the long winter nights, deprived of company, they spend their evenings reading at the corner of the hearth the entertaining books which they happen to get. In their primitive simplicity, they are not concerned with literature nor with witticism; they read to break up their monotony and not to instruct themselves; moral and philosophical works are as though they were nonexistent for them; such works would be of no use to them; they would never reach them. However, far from offering anything appropriate to them, your novels serve no other purpose than to make their situation more bitter for them. They alter their retreat into a frightful desert, and for the few hours of distraction which they are given, novels prepare months of unrest and vain regrets for them. Why wouldn't I dare to claim that, by some happy turn of fate, this book, just like so many other worse ones, can come into the hands of these country people, and that the image of joys of a situation quite similar to theirs will make it more bearable? I like to picture two spouses reading this collection together, finding in it new courage with which to bear their common tasks, and new insights to make them appear useful. How could they contemplate the scene of a happy household without wanting to imitate such a sweet model? How will they be moved by the charm of the marital state, even without the presence of love, without their own being tightened and strengthened? After their reading, they will not be saddened by their condition, nor discouraged by their cares. On the contrary, everything around them will assume a happier face; their duties will increase in dignity for them; they will rediscover the tastes for the pleasures of nature; its true feelings will be reborn in their hearts, and, seeing happiness within their reach, they will learn to use it. They will fulfill the same obligations; but they will fulfill them with a different soul, and will do as true patriarchs what they used to do as peasants.

N.   Up to this point, everything is all right. Husbands, wives, mothers of families. . . . But girls: have you nothing to say about them?

R.   No. A decent girl does not read any love stories at all. If the one who reads this one complains of the harm it will have done her, she is lying. The harm was done earlier. She has nothing more to lose.

N.   Magnificent! Pornographic authors: come into the classroom! You have all been justified.

R.   Yes, if they are justified by their own personal feelings and by the purpose of their writings.

N.   Are you the same under these conditions?

R.   I am too proud to answer that; but Julie made a rule for judging books for herself (reference to Part II, Letter 18 of *La Nouvelle Héloïse*); if you find it to be good, use it to judge this one. Attempts have been made to make the reading of novels useful to young people. I know of no plan which is more absurd. It is the same thing as cutting off your nose to spite your face. According to this mad idea, instead of aiming the moral purpose of these works at its goal, this message is always addressed to girls, while forgetting that these girls play no part in the disorders which are complained of. In general, their behavior is correct, although their hearts may be corrupt. They obey their mothers while waiting for the opportunity to imitate them. When women do their duty, you can be sure that girls will not fail in theirs.

N.   Observation contradicts you in this regard. It appears that a certain period of moral laxity is necessary to the sexes, in one social condition or another. It is a bad germ which sooner or later ferments. Among moral nations, the girls are lax and the women strict; the opposite is found in nations which are not. The former are concerned only with offenses, and the latter only with scandal. It is a simple question of being protected from temptations; crime does not enter into it at all.

R.   If one views the consequences, one would not come to that conclusion. But let us be fair toward women; the cause of their disorder resides less within themselves than in our corrupt institutions.

Since all of the sentiments of nature are suppressed by extreme inequality, it is from the iniquitous tyranny of fathers that children's vices and misfortunes come; it is with compulsory and badly arranged ties that young women, victims of the avarice and vanity of their parents, remove the scandal of their earlier decency by some misbehavior in which they revel. Do you seek to cure the evil? Then go directly to its source. If there is some reform to be undertaken in public behavior, it should begin with domestic behavior, and this depends totally on fathers and mothers. But this is not the means of controlling instruction; your licentious authors never preach except to those who are oppressed; and the moral lesson of books will always remain futile, because it is nothing more than the art of courting the most powerful.

N.   Surely your own moral lesson is not slavish; but to the degree that we are free, are we not excessively free? Is it enough for your morality to go to the source of the evil? Are you not afraid that it might do some evil itself?

R.   Evil? To whom? In times of contagious diseases and epidemics, when everyone is susceptible from the moment of birth, do people limit the distribution of good drugs to the ill on the basis that they might be harmful to the healthy? Sir, we differ so greatly on this point, that if there is any hope for the success of these letters, I am most convinced that they will do more good than a superior book.

N.   It is true that you have an excellent woman for a preacher. I am delighted to see you reconciled with women; I was angered that you forbade them to preach sermons to us.

R. You are pressing me on; I must stop speaking; I am neither foolish nor wise enough to be constantly right. Let us leave these bones to be picked over by the critics.

N. Gladly, for fear that critics might not have enough. But would there be nothing else to say to others about all the rest, about how one would pass on to the strict censor of the theater the vivid situations and animated sentiments which fill this collection? Show me one drama scene which equals those of the grove at Clarens and the dressing room. Reread the letter on spectacles; reread this collection. . . . Be consistent, or give up your rules. . . . What do you want people to think?

R. Sir, I want a critic to be consistent himself; and I do not want him to judge before he examines. Reread the work which you just quoted more closely; reread also the preface to *Narcisse;* in it you will find an answer to the inconsistency of which you accuse me. The fools who claim to have found them in *Le Devin du village* will assuredly find many more here. They will do what they must; but you. . . .

N. I recall two passages. . . . You do not greatly respect your contemporaries.

R. Sir, I am their contemporary, also! Oh! Why was I not born in an age where I should have burned these writings!

N. You exaggerate, as is your custom; but your precepts are rather accurate to a certain point. For example, if your Heloise had always been wise, she would instruct people much less; for whom would she serve as a model? During the most corrupt eras people prefer the most perfect moral lessons. Thus they are excused from practicing them; and by idle reading, a slight remnant of virtue is satisfied.

R. Sublime authors, bring your models down to a lower level, if you seek to have them imitated. To whom do you vaunt a purity that has not been stained? Tell us instead of a purity which can be regained; perhaps someone will be able to at least understand you.

N.   Your young hero made these observations already; but, no matter; you will be found no less guilty for having said what one does, in order to point out later what should have been done. And this does not even include the fact that to inspire love in girls and prudence in women is to reverse the established order of things, and brings back that little moral lesson that philosophy has outlawed. Whatever you say, love among girls is indecent and scandalous, and only a husband can approve of a lover. What a strange clumsiness to be indulgent toward the girls who are not supposed to read you, and harsh toward the women who will judge you. Believe me: if you fear your success, be calm; your steps were too well taken for you to fear such an effrontery. Whatever it may be, I will protect your secret; you need not be totally imprudent. If you believe that you are introducing a useful book, that is fine; but do not admit it.

R.   Not admit it, sir? Does a decent man conceal himself when he speaks to the public? Does he dare print what he would not claim as his own? I am the editor of this book, and I will present myself in it as editor.

N.   You will name yourself? You?

R.   Exactly.

N.   What! You will put your name on it?

R.   Yes.

N.   Your true name? *Jean-Jacques Rousseau,* written out completely?

R.   *Jean-Jacques Rousseau,* written out in full.

N.   You do not understand! what will they say about you?

R.   Whatever they wish. I place my name at the beginning of this work not to associate it to me, but to account for it. If there are bad elements in it, they should be imputed to me. If it contains any good, I do not intend to flatter myself over it. If the book is considered to be inherently bad, that is one more reason for me to sign it. I do not seek to be anything better than

I really am.

N.   Are you satisfied with this answer?

R.   Yes, in an age when it is impossible for anyone to be good.

N.   And the truly fine people, did you forget them?

R.   Nature created them, your institutions spoil them.

N.   At the beginning of a love story, these words will be read: By *J. J. ROUSSEAU, Citizen of Geneva*?

R.   *Citizen of Geneva*? I do not slander the name of my country; I put it only on writings which I consider capable of doing honor to it.

N.   You bear yourself a name which is not without honor, and you also have something to lose. You are introducing a weak and shallow book which will harm you. I would like to prevent you from doing it; but if you follow through with the stupidity, I agree that it may as well be done publicly and candidly. That will at least conform to your character. By the way, will you also put your motto on this book?

R.   My bookseller already played this joke on me, and I consider it so apt, that I promised to honor him with it. No, sir, I will not place my motto on this book; but I will not abandon it simply for that, and I fear now less than ever for having adopted it. You recall that I considered having these letters printed when I wrote against spectacles, and that the need to justify one of these writings did not force me to alter the truth of the other. I admit in advance that I bear perhaps more guilt than I will be accused of. He who likes the truth more than his personal glory can also like it more than his own life. You always want men to be consistent; I doubt that men are capable of it; but what they are capable of is always being true; that is what I want to try to be.

N.   When I ask you if you are the author of these letters, why then do you evade my question?

R.   For the very fact that I do not wish to tell a lie.

N.   But you also refuse to tell the truth.

R.   I am paying it an honor when I say that I will keep it silent. You would do better to deal with a man who would prefer to lie. Besides, are people of good taste fooled by authors' pens?   How do you dare ask a question which you yourself should answer?

N.   I would answer it well for some of these letters; they certainly were written by you; but I no longer recognize you in the others, and I doubt that one can disguise oneself to this extent.   Nature, which does not fear any misrepresentation, often changes its appearance, while the trick involved is revealed in the effort to be more natural than nature itself; an example is the grumbler of the animal fable who does the animal's voice better than the animal itself. This collection is filled with awkwardnesses that the worst scribbler would have avoided. The oratory, repetitions, contradictions, perpetual redundancy; what man could do better and yet would decide to do it so poorly?   What man would have kept the shocking proposal to Julie by that insane Edouard?   What man would not have corrected the absurdity of the little simpleton who, whenever he wants to die, goes to the bother of letting the whole world know about it, and yet who enjoys good health at the end? What man would not have begun by saying to himself: the characters have to be carefully separated; their styles must be precisely varied?   Inevitably he would have fared better in this project than nature itself.

I notice that in a very intimate society, styles approximate one another as do characters, and that friends confuse one another's soul as well as their manners of thinking, feeling and speaking. Your Julie, such as she is, must be an enchanting creature; all that comes close to her must resemble her; everything which surrounds Julie must become Julie; all of her friends can have but one tone; but these things make themselves felt, they are not created. If they were, the creator would not dare to put them in practice. All that is required are general characteristics; what becomes simple through subtlety is of no more use to him. Now that is where the stamp of truth is; that is the place where an attentive eye seeks and finds nature.

R.   Well then, what is your conclusion?

N.   I have none; I doubt, and I really do not know how to explain it to you, how much this doubt tormented me during the reading of these letters.   Surely if all this is nothing more than fiction, you have written a bad book; but tell me that these two women actually lived, and I will reread this collection every year till the end of my life.

R.   What does it matter whether they lived?   You would search for them on this earth in vain.   They are no longer alive.

N.   No longer alive? Then they did live once?

R.   That conclusion is conditional: if they once were alive, they are no more.

N.   Just between us, admit that these little subleties are more positive than bothersome.

R.   They are what you insist that they be, so that I will be neither revealed nor forced to lie.

N.   My word, your effort will be of no use, you will be identified anyway.   Do you not see that your epigraph says everything by itself?

R.   I do see that it says nothing about the question at hand; who can be sure if I found this epigraph in the manuscript, or if I added it myself.   Who can say if I do not share the same doubts as yours?   Or if all this aura of mystery perhaps is not a cloak for hiding from you my own ignorance of what you seek to know.

N.   But at least you are familiar with the locale.   Have you been to Vevay? to the Vaud area?

R.   Several times, and I assure you that I never heard talk of the Baron d'Etange nor of his daughter there.   The name of Wolmar is totally unknown there.   I have been to Clarens: I found nothing similar to the house described in these letters. While returning from Italy, I passed through it the very year of the terrible event, and as far as I know, no one wept over Julie de Wolmar, nor anything resembling it. Finally, to the best of my recollection of the land, I noticed transformations of the places and geographical mistakes in these letters; it could have been that the author knows no better, or that he sought to disorientate his readers. There is all that you will learn from me on this point, and rest assured that no one else will learn from me what I refused to tell you.

N.   Everyone will have the same curiosity as I. If you publish this work, then tell people what you told me. Even better, use this conversation as your only preface; all the necessary explanations are in it.

R.   You are right: it is better than anything I would have written. Besides, these types of apologies scarcely ever succeed.

N.   No, when it is seen that the author protects himself; but I was careful so that this weakness not be found in this one. I merely advise you to reverse the roles. Pretend that it was I who urge you to publish this collection, and that you refuse to. You give the objections, and I will give the answers. That will be more modest and will have a better effect.

R.   Will this also be in conformance with what you praised to me earlier?

N.   No, I was setting a trap for you. Leave things as they are.

VII
DIDEROT: PRAISE OF THE ENGLISH NOVEL

Diderot's concept of the novel is as complicated as this man of genius was himself. His three major works of prose fiction, *Les Bijoux indiscrets* (1748), *La Religieuse* (1760), and *Jacques le fataliste* (1773-75), form one of the most incohesive groups imaginable. Among the French novelists previously considered, critical and theoretical material has usually been confined to a few prefaces or journalistic sources. Diderot's treatment of the genre is diffused throughout his entire work.[1]

In further contrast to the authors previously examined, most of whom evolved away from a condemnatory view of the novel and toward a favorable one, Diderot experienced a complete or 360-degree evolution in attitude. He began by denouncing the novel and ended his career with those initial opinions. In between, however, he was an ardent admirer of the realist novel, both domestic and foreign, his own and those of other authors. These three different attitudinal phases can be further differentiated as follows. The first segment of his career would include the early works up to 1750, after which the enormous enterprise of *L'Encyclopédie* occupied most of his time and attention. Here, *Les Bijoux indiscrets* typifies Diderot's low opinion of prose fiction. The second and more mature period lasts from 1750 to 1761, and is characterized by a temporary flirtation with conventions, in the novel as well as in drama, and the relationship between art and morality. *La Religieuse* is, of course, the product of this era, and *L'Eloge de Richardson* constitutes a manifesto of this period of the conventional, moral novel (it is provided as an appendix). The last decades of Diderot's life are concerned with an "abstract" novel, *Jacques le fataliste,* whose form is radically different from that of its predecessor, *La Religieuse,* and shows a gradual detachment of morality from art in Diderot's doctrine.[2]

In examining Diderot's novels, one very important often-neglected fact should be recalled: the majority of his fictional works were virtually *unknown* during his lifetime. *Les Bijoux indiscrets* was sufficiently provocative to merit its author a stay in the Vincennes prison; but the more significant ones, *La Religieuse*, (written in 1760, published in 1796) and *Jacques le fataliste* (written between 1773 and 1775, published in France only in 1796), were unknown to the contemporary public, and did not therefore have any direct influence on subsequent productions in the genre. As Dieckmann points out, the Diderot of the eighteenth century was known as the *encyclopédiste*, the dramatist and the art critic, not as a novelist.[3] His reputation was thus largely determined by posterity.

Chronology tells us that Diderot was in a position to provide an overview of the majority of French Enlightenment novels. Unfortunately, his views contain hardly any more praise than did the views of the preceding novelists reflecting on the romances of the seventeenth century. In 1781 he remarked to his daughter: "I have always treated novels as rather frivolous creations."[4] It would appear that, according to Diderot, little progress had been achieved in the novel since its beginning.

It is mildly surprising that Diderot, the author of *Les Bijoux indiscrets*, had very little to say concerning Montesquieu's *Lettres persanes*, since both works were *romans à clef*, laden with ill-disguised barbs against the French monarchy and administration. In a letter to Grimm dated March 25, 1781, Diderot referred to *Les Lettres persanes* as "une erreur de jeunesse" ("a youthful mistake") made by Montesquieu, and added that this mistake had been atoned for by *De L'Esprit des Lois*.[5]

Montesquieu had less to atone for in his youthful caprices. The narrative situation in *Les Bijoux indiscrets* is reminiscent of Crébillon's *Sopha*. Mangogul, the Sultan of *Le Congo*, sought to obtain some very confidential information from the female members of his court. To do this, he consulted the genie Cucufa, who gave him a magic ring which, when turned toward the women, would make the most private parts of their anatomy speak. Whereas Diderot lamented frivolity and indecency in other authors, he also regretted *Les Bijoux indiscrets*. He made an observation to his friend and publisher Naigeon which places this type of fiction in the proper perspective:

> Bad books do not create bad morals in a people, but their
> bad morals do create bad books; they are like the fetid
> smells from a cloaca.[6]

Diderot had a rather low opinion of Marivaux; in several instances, he satirized the author of *Le Paysan Parvenu* and *La Vie de Marianne:* "And may nine thousand devils carry off Mariveau (sic) and all his insipid imitators such as myself."[7] The date of this letter (1760) is significant, since Diderot's own works of that era did resemble Marivaux's. Although he rejected Marivaux's early adventure tales, the two novelists were not that different in terms of the importance given to language and style in literature.[8]

Diderot had little to say concerning Rousseau's *Nouvelle Héloïse.* There are several letters to Rousseau in the *Correspondance générale* in which Diderot apologized for not having had the time to read Rousseau's manuscript, as the latter had requested. There remains the remark in Book IX of Rousseau's *Confessions,* where the latter summarized Diderot's attitude toward *La Nouvelle Héloïse* as being "stuffed," and the argument over superiority revolving around Samuel Richardson.

Diderot's view of Prévost shows an interesting evolution, one which coincides with Diderot's general attitude toward the novel. In the *Discours de la Poésie dramatique* (1758), Diderot praised the sentimental and moral powers of the author of the *Mémoires et aventures d'un homme de qualité:*

> Each line of *l'Homme de qualité retiré du monde,* of the
> *Doyen de Killerine,* and of *Cleveland,* arouses in me a
> movement of interest for the misfortunes of virtue, and
> causes me to shed tears. What art would be more loath-
> some than the one which would make me a partisan of
> vice?[9]

Here, Diderot praised Prévost for many of the same merits that he saw in Richardson. But by the time of *Jacques le fataliste,* his esteem of Prévost had vanished: "I could have called someone to help him; it would have been a member of his own company, but that would have reeked to high heaven of Cleveland."[10] The Diderot who praised Prévost in 1758 is the Diderot of *La Religieuse,* while the Diderot who condemned false realism in *Cleveland* was the hater of the novel and the author of the anti-novel, *Jacques le fataliste.*

The same negative attitudes toward the French novel reappear in chapter XLVI of *Les Bijoux indiscrets* and again in a letter to his daughter Angélique on July 28, 1781, where the father prescribed a cure for his wife's vapors. Since his wife had been reading *Gil Blas,* Diderot recommended:

> . . .eight pages of the *Roman comique;* four chapters of *Don Quixote;* a well-selected paragraph from Rabelais; blend all of that into a reasonable quantity of *Jacques le fataliste,* or *Manon Lescaut,* and alternate these drugs as you would with herbs, by replacing them with others which are worth about as much.[11]

Of note is that the "pharmacist" did not hesitate to include his own *Jacques le fataliste* in the concoction of boring fiction.

With few exceptions, Diderot's opinions such as the above underwent little change during the rest of his life. The modern reader would expect to find a less severe treatment of masterpieces like *Manon Lescaut.* Even if we allow for moments of innocent jest, Diderot remained a hater of the vast majority of French novels. The sole great exception to the commonly-held notion of *le roman* would remain an Englishman.

Before passing to that great exception, a few remarks concerning Diderot's best-known novel, *La Religieuse,* are in order. When compared to the diffuse and obscene *Bijoux indiscrets, La Religieuse* is simplicity itself. It is not enough, however, to describe it merely as a conventional memoir novel in which the main character supposedly narrates his or her life story; the point of departure of *La Religieuse* was an elaborate hoax, or *mystification,* played on a friend by Diderot.

The source of this hoax is found in an extract written apparently by Grimm in the *Correspondence littéraire* in 1770.[12] (In fact, the novel itself was first released to the subscribers of the *Correspondance littéraire,* like *Jacques le fataliste.*) According to Grimm, the Marquis de Croismare, a very dear friend to Diderot, Grimm, and the *encyclopédistes,* left Paris for his home in Caen in 1759. In order to solicit the return of this dear friend, Crois-

mare, to Paris, a scheme was devised, with Diderot as the principle plotter. The latter knew that Croismare had taken particular
interest in the case of a real nun who, in 1758, had attempted to
obtain release from the vows binding here to a convent against
her will. This nun was Marguerite Delamarre, whose case fur-
nished the material for Diderot's novel.[13] Since Croismare had
already expressed an acute interest in the case, Diderot composed
a series of letters, supposedly written by the actual nun in question, begging for Croismare's intercession on her behalf. These
letters constitute what is known as the *Préface-Annexe de la
Religieuse.*

In order to make the letters appear as authentic as possible,
Diderot made several purposeful mistakes at the onset: Croismare's name was mispelled, and the first letter was sent to the
Ecole Royale Militaire, instead of to Caen. Approximately twenty letters were exchanged between the real Marquis de Croismare
and the fictitious nun, including several from a Mme Moreau-
Madin, who served as Diderot's intermediary in the correspondence. The hoax was brought to a premature finish in May,
1760, when Croismare became so interested in "Suzanne
Simonin" that he prepared a place for her as governess of his
daughter, who was at the time residing in a convent. Consequently, Diderot had his imaginary Suzanne die. When Croismare was eventually informed of the prank played on him by his
friends, he merely laughed, according to Grimm, and his friendship with Diderot was none the worse for it.

Although two different texts are involved, the relationship
between *La Religieuse* and the prankish letters is as follows:
since the letters which form the *Préface-Annexe* were printed in
the *Correspondance littéraire* in 1770, they were known before
the actual novel, which was not released to the subscribers until
1780-1782.   Secondly, the letters were made known to the
general public in the first edition by Jacques Buisson in 1796.
This indiscretion was sorely regretted by the second editor of *La
Religieuse,* Naigeon, who feared unfavorable reactions from the
public, since the proverbial cat had been let out of the bag.
Thirdly, numerous overlappings and parallels between the
Préface-Annexe and the novel occur; for example the first letter
from Suzanne Simonin to Croismare (*OEuvres,* p. 1387), where
she enumerates her qualifications, is, with a few changes of word
order, almost identical to the listings by Suzanne Simonin of the

novel (*OEuvres,* p. 392).

Naigeon's reservations point directly to the central problem of *La Religieuse* and of one concerning Diderot's fictional works in general—the relationship between truth and fiction. Without the *Préface-Annexe,* the novel would have retained its full impact as an authenticated case history, due to the fact that a real nun had made her situation known in the 1750's. But with the premature appearance of this document, the novel places itself in a nebulous, ill-defined zone between fact and fiction. Diderot was intentionally ambiguous, a *mystificateur,* as Catrysse calls him.[14]   For this author, the difference between a fictional "story" presented as authentic, and a true story transcribed into fiction is minimal.

Diderot analyzed *La Religieuse* in several instances in his correspondence. The major account reads as follows:

> It (*La Religieuse*) is the counterpart of *Jacques le fataliste.* It is replete with pathetic scenes. It is very interesting, and all the attention is focused on the character who speaks. I am sure that it will touch your readers more than *Jacques* made them laugh, which results in the possibility that they may prefer its ending. It is entitled *La Religieuse,* and I do not feel that a more frightful satire of convents has ever been written.[15]

This excerpt reveals the new dimension of Diderot as a novelist: that of propagandist. In view of the sadistic and excessive sufferings of Suzanne, the author is testing the convent system in France to the limit. This message reaches a peak of intensity in the novel: "Kill your daughter rather than locking her up in a convent against her wishes; yes, kill her" (*OEuvres,* p. 296).

Diderot wrote *L'Eloge de Richardson* in 1761, and he wrote it in one day. His selection of Richardson as the only expression of art in the novel is striking in itself. It is indeed a sad testament to the French novel, when Diderot calls for a term other than *novel* to be applied to *Pamela, Clarissa,* and *Sir Charles Grandison.*   The exclamatory and extremely profuse praise lavished on Richardson may be due to the haste with which it was written; be that as it may, the document is quite clear as to what Diderot expected to find in a good novel at this stage in his evolution.

Richardson's novels represented the epitome of realism in the eyes of Diderot, especially when compared to the other strings of "frivolous and imaginary events": "The essence of his drama is truth, his characters are reality incarnate; their behavior is taken from actual society; his events can be found in the customs of all civilized nations. . ." For Diderot, Richardson portrayed that type of reality found in daily life, not that of princes and princesses, savages and monsters. The comment also applies to Diderot's justification of Richardsonian length in the novel; Diderot sought and found in him the portrait of life which he could envision for himself.

This principle of artistic truth was so accurate for Diderot that he went so far as to prefer Richardson's fiction to truth itself: "Oh Richardson, I dare say that the truest of histories is filled with lies, whereas your novel is filled with truth." Keeping in mind that the very notion of history was in a state of evolution in the Enlightenment, Diderot's scorn for it could be explained by the inaccuracies and subjectivity used by contemporary historians. Of note is the exactly opposite point of view found in Prévost, and the precedence of fiction over history found here.

At this moment in the development of his artistic values, Diderot sought and praised realism not only in the English novel, but in painting and drama as well. His eulogy of Chardin in the *Salon de 1763* is similar in tone, impression and message to the *Eloge de Richardson:*

> On Chardin! it is not the white, red and black colors
> which you mingle on your palette; it is the very substance
> of the objects, it is the appearance and the manner which
> you capture on the tip of your brush and put on the canvas.[16]

Chardin was an excellent choice for conveying what Diderot considered to be truth in art. His tableaux, such as *La Pourvoyeuse* and *Le Bénédicté* are striking in their earthiness and the sobriety of their subjects. They aroused in Diderot the sentiment of nature itself, as he intended the novel to do.

Two other qualities of Samuel Richardson contributed to his superiority in the eyes of Diderot. They were his powers of creating a visual image in the mind of the reader:

> I have formed an image of the characters put on stage by the author; their faces are there; I recognize them in the street, in the town squares, in houses; I am drawn toward or away from them. One of the advantages of his work is that having covered a vast area, some part of his tableau constantly remains visible in my eyes.

and the powers of Richardson as a *moralist*. Strange as it may seem from the author of *Les Bijoux indiscrets* and the burlesque scenes in *Jacques le fataliste,* the novelist had to be a moralist as well as a painter and dramatist. Diderot noted the failure of the conventional moralists (Montaigne, Charron, La Rochefoucauld and Nicole) because their maxims remained in the realm of the abstract. In contrast, Richardson had rendered the abstract into concrete action; his works were morality *par excellence,* which permitted the reader to witness the development of virtue:

> Richardson sows in our hearts the seeds of virtue which initially remain dormant and tranquil; they stay there until the opportunity presents itself for their agitation and expansion. Then they develop; we feel that we are brought to do good with a fugue which we have never experienced before. Confronted with injustice, we feel a repugnance which we could not explain.

Diderot did not state explicitly why he considered Prévost, Rousseau, and other French novelists as having failed in the area of morality. We have already witnessed their adamant claims to that effect. But by their omission, and by the insistence on Richardson as the unique expression of morality in the novel, those claims apparently did not impress Diderot at all.

The era of *La Religieuse* and *L'Eloge de Richardson,* roughly 1750 to 1763, represents that period where morality was an integral part of Diderot's concept of literature. Further evidence of this principle is found in the *Discours de la poésie dramatique* (1758):

> Oh what goodness would befall men, if all of the arts

were to propose a common goal for themselves, and would one day compete with laws to make us love virtue and detest vice! The philosopher is the one who should invite them to do it; it is up to him to address the poet, the musician and the painter, and shout to them forcefully: Men of genius: why have you been gifted by the heavens?[17]

This invocation in favor of a community of the arts and the role of the philosopher who should lead such an effort is further denunciation of the works of Diderot's compatriots in the novel, several of whom were also philosophers.

A brief mention of *Jacques le fataliste*, Diderot's third significant contribution to French prose fiction of the Enlightenment, is warranted. It is truly the "counterpart of *La Religieuse*," as Diderot stated in a letter to Meister on September 27, 1780, and which he had recommended as a cure for vapors in a letter to his daughter on July 28, 1781. These dates are important because Diderot's attitude underwent total change from the 1750-1760 decade. *Jacques le fataliste* is another theoretical text; it abounds in criticism of the novel, negativity toward itself and other works, fragmentary episodes and questions for which there are no answers. The first paragraph of the work is exemplary of what follows:

How did they meet? By chance, like everybody. What were their names? What difference does it make to you? Where were they from? From the nearest place. Where were they going? Do people always know where they are going? What were they saying? The master said nothing, and Jacques said that his captain used to say that all the good and bad things which happen to us down here were written up there.

This refusal to establish a mood or a stage, when one is expected, reflects an acute disenchantment with regular approaches to fiction. It is a further rejection by Diderot of the attempt to pass off the false as if it were the truth. In *Jacques*, he made no effort to conceal his parody of yet another parody, Sterne's *Tristram Shandy*. Within this dislocated framework, there are some "regular" narrative scenes, and some magnificent ones (e.g., the story of Madame de la Pommeraye and *le père* Hudson). But in general, the work follows any direction which happened to come to mind to the author.

Once again, evidence is found for this change of view in Diderot's other critical writings. In the *Salons* of 1763 and 1767, he criticized Boucher and Hubert Robert respectively for excessive details, the art which he had so admired in Richardson. When Diderot did present detailed description in *Jacques*, he would often ridicule the reader, such as in the beginning of the story of the Marquis des Arcis and Madame de la Pommerays (see *OEuvres*, p. 581).

Later, Diderot apologized for not providing more connections between the characters he had randomly selected:

> A writer of novels would not have failed to do so, but I do not like novels, except for those of Richardson. I write the story: this story will be interesting or uninteresting; that is the least of my worries. My goal is to be true, and I have fulfilled it (*OEuvres*, p. 670).

It should not be concluded from the preceding discussion that there is no art in Diderot's prose fiction after 1760. On the contrary, his techniques in *Le Neveu de Rameau* and *Jacques le fataliste* are more appreciated today than the traditional approach found in *La Religieuse*. In these innovative works of the 1770 decade, Diderot tended away from tradition and toward artifice. In *Le Neveu de Rameau*, the forces of *bienfaisance* and *malfaisance* engage in struggle which unfolds before the reader's eyes; the traditional victory of the former remains uncertain. *Jacques le fataliste* is the least traditional representation of life, because human life and behavior do not follow structured, regular patterns. They are beset with pedestrain and irregular interferences. This approximation of reality in fiction, according to Diderot's own concept of the term, and in spite of his contempt for *les romans*, constitutes the most avant-garde effort in the eighteenth-century French novel. The complicated collaboration of author and reader is, as Diderot would have wanted it, more similar to the techniques used since Gide and the French novelists of the 1960 generation, than to the conventional *novel* of Diderot's own time.

NOTES

[1]Roger Kempf, *Diderot et le roman* (Paris: Seuil, 1964), p. 10.

[2]My main edition for Diderot's works is that of André Billy in the *Bibliothèque de la Pléiade* (Paris: Gallimard, 1951), referred to parenthetically as *OEuvres*. I occasionally cite the Assézat-Tourneux edition of *OEuvres complètes* (Paris: Garnier, 1875-77), and refer to it by *A. T.* Finally, for Diderot's correspondence, I used the edition of G. Roth and J. Varloot (Paris: Editions de Minuit, 1955-70), and refer to it as *C. G.* All translations are my own.

[3]Henri Dieckmann, *Cinq Leçons sur Diderot* (Geneva: Droz, 1959), p. 17.

[4]*C. G.*, vol. XV, p. 190.

[5]*C. G.*, vol. XV, p. 215.

[6]*A. T.*, vol. IV, pp. 134-35.

[7]Letter to Sophie Volland, November, 1760, in *C. G.*, vol. III, p. 230.

[8]See Diderot's *Lettre sur les aveugles,* in *A. T.*, vol. I, pp. 301-302, where he refers specifically to Marivaux.

[9]*A. T.*, vol. VII, p. 313.

[10]*OEuvres*, pp. 503-04.

[11]*C. G.*, vol. XV, p. 254.

[12]The extract does not appear in Maurice Tourneux's edition of *Correspondance littéraire.* The version discussed here is found in Billy's edition of Diderot's *OEuvres*.

[13]See Georges May, *Diderot et la Religieuse* (New Haven, Conn.: Yale University Press, 1964), ch. III.

[14]Jean Catrysse, *Diderot et la mystification* (Paris: Nizet, 1970).

[15]*C. G.,* vol. XV, pp. 190-91.

[16]Diderot, *Salon de 1763,* in *OEuvres complètes,* ed. of Le Club français du livre, vol, V, p. 432.

[17]Diderot, *Discours de la Poésie dramatique,* in *A. T.,* vol. VII, p. 313.

DIDEROT: APPENDIX
ELOGE DE RICHARDSON (1761)

Up till now, people have understood by the term *novel* a string of frivolous and imaginary events, the reading of which was dangerous for good taste and morals. I would prefer that another name be found for Richardson's works, which elevate the mind, move the soul, exude the love of good everywhere, and which are also called novels.

Everything which was put into maxims by Montaigne, Charron, La Rochefoucauld and Nicole, Richardson has put it into action. But an intelligent man, who reads Richardson's works thoughtfully, rephrases most of the moralists' maxims; and with all of these rules, he could not improve on one single page of Richardson.

A maxim is an abstract and general rule for behavior whose application is left up to us. In itself, it does not imprint any sensitive image in our mind; but someone who acts can be seen, and people can place themselves in his situation or by his side; they become animated for or against him; they identify with his role, if he is virtuous; if he is unjust or corrupt, they withdraw from him indignantly. What person did not tremble at the character of a Lovelace or a Tomlinson? Who was not struck with horror by the true and pathetic tone, by the air of candor and dignity, by the penetrating skill with which the latter depicts all virtues? What person has not said to himself deep in his heart that he should flee from society and seek refuge in the depths of the wilderness, if there exists a certain number of such deceitful men?

Oh Richardson! we become involved in your works, willingly or not; we become involved in the conversations, we agree, we accuse, we admire, we become irritated or angry. So many times have I caught myself, just as it happens to children taken to see a performance for the first time, yelling: "Don't believe him, he is tricking you. . . If you go there, you are lost." My soul was kept in a constant state of agitation. How good I was! How just I was! How satisfied I was with myself! When I finished reading you, I was the same as a man who has spent an entire day doing good works.

In the span of a few hours, I had gone through a great number of situations that the longest of lives would present in its entire duration. I had heard true discussions of passion; I had witnessed the motives of self-interest and of self-esteem operating in a hundred different manners; I had become a spectator to a throng of incidents, and I felt that I had acquired some experience.

This writer does not have blood dripping from the walls; he does not transport you into distant lands; he does not subject you to cannibals; he does not lurk in clandestine houses of debauchery; he is never lost in fairy-tale lands. He is to be found in the world in which we live; the essence of his drama in truth, his characters are reality incarnate; their behavior is taken from actual society; his events can be found in the customs of all civilized nations; the passions he portrays are the same that I feel inside me; the same objects motivate them, they have the strength which I know to be proper to them; the tribulations and afflictions of his characters are of the same nature as those which trouble me incessantly; he shows me the general pattern of things which surround me. Without this art, the illusion would be merely temporary, the effect would be weak and fleeting, and my soul would be painfully bent along capricious winding paths.

What is virtue? By whatever facet it is examined, it is a sacrifice of oneself. The self-sacrifice which happens as an idea is a preconceived inclination to self-sacrifice in reality.

Richardson sows in our hearts the seeds of virtue which initially remain dormant and tranquil; they stay there until the opportunity presents itself for their agitation and expansion. Then they develop; we feel that we are brought to do good with a fugue which we have never experienced before. Confronted with injustice, we feel a repugnance which we could not explain. This is because we have encountered Richardson; it is because we have conversed with a good man in times when our unselfish souls were open to the truth.

I still remember the first time when my hands came in contact with Richardson's works: it was in the country. How delightfully was I affected by reading them! Each moment, I felt that my happiness was cut short by the turning of a page. I soon experienced the same sensation felt by a group of perfectly compatible men who might have lived together for a long time and who would be departing. Suddenly, in the end, I felt that I was left entirely alone.

This writer always brings us back to the important things in life. The more we read him, the more pleasure we take in reading him.

It is he who illuminates the inner reaches of the cavern; it is he who teaches us to discern those subtle and dishonest motives which hide behind other honest motives, ones which hasten to reveal themselves first. He breathes on the sublime phantom at the cavern's entrance; and the hideous Moor which it concealed now becomes visible.

It is he who makes our passions speak, at times with that violence which can no longer be repressed, at other times with that affected and moderate tone which they assume in different circumstances.

It is he who makes men of all levels, of all social conditions, and of all of life's varied situations, speak in a language which we recognize. If there is a secret sentiment in the innermost part of the soul of a character he introduces, listen closely and you will hear a discordant sound which reveals it. This is because Richardson has understood that lies can never completely resemble truth, because truth is truth, whereas lies remain lies.

If, aside from any considerations beyond this life, it is important for men to be persuaded that we have nothing more to do to insure our happiness that to be virtuous, what a great service has been done by Richardson for mankind! He has not defined this truth; but he has made it felt: in every line, he makes us prefer the lot of virtue oppressed to that of vice triumphant. Who would want to be Lovelace with all his assets? Who would not want to be Clarissa, in spite of all her misfortunes?

Often have I said while reading him: "I would gladly give my life to be like her; I would rather be dead than to be like him."

If, in spite of the motives which could interfere with my good judgment, I know how to distribute scorn or respect with the right degree of impartiality, I owe it to Richardson. Read him again, my friends, and you will no longer misconstrue those little qualities which are of use to you; you will no longer weaken the great talents which cross or humble you.

Men, come learn from him how to cope with the evils in life; come, together we shall weep over the unfortunate characters in his writings, and we shall say: "If fate overwhelms us, at least noble people will in turn weep over us." If Richardson has attempted to persuade anyone, it was in favor of the unfortunate. In his work, just as in the real world, men are divided into two groups: those who enjoy and those who suffer. It is always with the latter group that he places me; and without my being aware of it, a sentiment of compassion is effected and enhanced.

He has left me with a pleasing and enduring melancholy; sometimes it is apparent to others, and they ask me: "What is the matter? You are not acting naturally; what happened to you?" They ask me about my health, my financial situation, family and friends. O my dear friends! *Pamela, Clarissa* and *Grandison* are three great dramas! Torn away from this reading by serious preoccupations, I experienced a profound disgust; I left my duty aside, and I returned to Richardson's book. Be careful of opening these spellbinding works when duty calls.

Which of us has read Richardson's works without wanting to know this man, to have him as a brother or friend? Which of us has not wished all sorts of blessings for him?

Oh Richardson, Richardson, you are unique in my eyes, you will be my reading for all time to come. If I am forced by pressing needs, if a friend should fall into poverty, if my meager resources do not suffice to provide the necessities for my children's education, I will sell my books; but I will keep you, and keep you on the same shelf with Moses, Homer, Euripides and Sophocles, and I will read each of you in turn.

To the extent that one's soul is noble, that one's taste is delicate and pure, that one knows nature, and that one loves the truth, to that extent will Richardson's works be appreciated.

I have heard my author accused of lengthiness in his details: how troublesome were these accusations for me!

Woe to the man of genius who overcomes obstacles which habit and time have imposed on artistic production, and who tramples underfoot protocol and his guidelines! Many long years will pass by after his death before the justice which he deserves is given him.

Let us be fair, however. With a people bothered by countless distractions, where the day is not long enough for the amusements with which it is customarily filled, Richardson's books must seem long. It is for this same reason that the aforementioned people have an opera no more, and that in its other theaters only fragmented scenes from comedies and tragedies will always be presented.

My dear fellow countrymen, if Richardson's novels seem long to you, why do you not shorten them? Be logical. You hardly ever go to a tragedy except to see the final act. Skip immediately to the last twenty pages of *Clarissa*.

Richardson's details are unpleasant and should be unpleasant for a frivolous and dissolute man; but it was not for this man that he wrote; it was for a peaceful and solitary man, who knew the futility of the clatter and distraction of the world, and who prefers to live in a shadowy retreat, and be positively touched in silence.

You accuse Richardson of excessive length! You have forgotten how many pains, concerns and movements are required to make the least affair succeed, to conclude a marriage, or to bring about a reconciliation. You may think whatever you wish about these details; but they will be interesting to me, if they are true, if they reveal passions, if they portray characters.

They are common, you say; they can be seen every day! You are mistaken; they are the things that happen every day directly under your eyes, and which you never see. Be on guard;

you are arguing the case against the great poets and using the name of Richardson. You have seen the setting sun and the rising stars a hundred times; you have heard the countryside echo with the brilliant song of the birds; but who from among you felt that it was the day's noise which rendered the night's silence more touching? Well then! It is the same for you in moral phenomena as in physical phenomena: the emergence of passions often struck your ears; but you are far from understanding all of the hidden elements contained in their accents and expressions. Not one of them has its form; all of these forms follow one another on a single face, while the face remains the same; and the art of the great poet and great painter resides in showing you a furtive detail which has eluded you.

Painters, poets, men of taste, men of wealth, read Richardson; read him incessantly.

You must know that the illusion is based on this infinity of small things; it is difficult to imagine them; it is more difficult to create them. The gesture is sometimes as sublime as the spoken word; and then all of these detailed truths prepare the mind for striking impressions and great happenings. When your impatience is suspended by these temporary delays which serve it as barriers, with what impetuosity will it rise forth when the poet decides to remove the barriers. At that moment, when you are weakened with grief or overcome with joy, you will no longer have the strength to retain your tears and say to yourself: "But perhaps this is not true." This notion was gradually withdrawn from you; and it is so far removed that it will not reappear.

One idea which came to me while pondering Richardson's works, was that I had purchased an old manor; one day while visiting its rooms, I noticed in a corner a wardrobe which had not been opened for a long time, and when I forced it open, I imagined that I had haphazardly found the letters of Clarissa and Pamela. After having read a few, with what haste did I arrange them in their proper sequence! What sadness would have been mine, if there had been any gaps among them! Can you believe that I would have permitted a treacherous (I almost said sacrilegeous) hand to have omitted one single line?

Those of you who have read Richardson's works only in your elegant French translation, if you think you really know them, you are wrong.

You do not know Lovelace; you do not know Clementine; you do not know the unfortunate Clarissa; you do not know Miss Howe, her dear and loving Miss Howe, because you have not seen her dishevelled and stretched out on her friend's coffin, wringing her arms, raising her tearful eyes to the heavens, filling the Harlowe residence with her piercing cries, and making accusations against that entire cruel family; you are ignorant of the result of these instances which would be suppressed by your limited taste, since you did not hear the mournful sound of the parish bells, borne by the wind to the Harlowe house, and awakening in those hearts of stone their inert remorse, since you have not seen the shudders that they felt at the noise of the wheels of the funeral carriage which bore their victim. It was then that the sad silence which reigned in their midst was broken by the mother's and father's sobs; it was then that the true suffering of these wicked souls commenced, and that serpents gnawed at the depths of their hearts, and tore them asunder. Happy were those who could weep!

I have noticed that, in a group where Richardson was read individually or together, the conversation became more interesting and more vivid.

I have heard, during this reading, the most important aspects of morality and taste discussed and examined.

I have heard arguments about the behavior of its characters as though they were real events; there were praises and blames of Pamela, Clarissa, Grandison, as if they were living, identified beings in whom the greatest interest would have been taken.

Someone who was unfamiliar with the prior reading and who had led the discussion would have thought that it concerned a neighbor, friend, brother or sister, based on the truth and the liveliness of the conversation.

Shall I say it?. . . Due to the diversity of judgments, I have seen born latent hatred, hidden scorn—in short—the same divergences develop among compatible people, as though it concerned the gravest of matters. Then I compared Richardson's work to one that is even more sacred, to a gospel brought down to the earth to separate husband and wife, father and son, daughter and mother, brother and sister; and thus his work coincided with the situation of the most perfect of nature's beings. All having issued from an omnipotent and infinitely wise hand, not one of them has failed to sin in some instance. An element of good fortune at present can become the source of a great evil in the future; an evil, the source of good.

But what does it matter if, because of this author, I have come to love my equals and my duties more; if I have nothing more than pity for the wicked; if I feel more commiseration for the unfortunate, more respect for the good, more care in the exercise of things at hand, more indifference for future things, more scorn for life, and more love for virtue, which is the only good that we can request of heaven, and the only one that it can grant us for our indiscreet requests.

I know the Harlowe house as well as my own; my father's residence is no more familiar to me than Grandison's; I have formed an image of the characters put on stage by the author; their faces are there; I recognize them in the street, in the town squares, in houses; I am drawn toward or away from them. One of the advantages of his work is, that having covered a vast area, some part of his tableau constantly remains visible in my eyes. Rarely do I find six people assembled together, without associating some of his names with them. He turns me toward honest people; he leads me away from the wicked; he taught me how to recognize them by quick and subtle signs. He even guides me sometimes without my being aware of it.

Richardson's work will please all men more or less, in all ages and in all countries; but the number of readers who will appreciate their full value will never be great: too rigid a taste is required; and besides, the variety of events is such, the relationships so numerous, behavior so complex, so many things prepared, others rescued, so many faces, so many personalities! Scarcely had I finished the first few pages of *Clarissa* that I had already encountered fifteen or sixteen characters; soon that number doubled. There are as many as forty in *Grandison*; but what surprisingly confuses people is to find that each one of them has his own ideas, expressions and tone of voice; and how these ideas, expressions and tones vary according to circumstance, motivation and passion, just as diverse expressions of passion follow one another on the same human face. Any man with taste will not mistake a letter of Mrs. Norton for one belonging to one of Clarissa's aunts, nor an aunt's letter for another from Mrs. Howe, nor a note from Mrs. Howe for one from Mrs. Harlowe, although these personages might share the same locale and sentiments relative to the same subject. In this immortal book as in springtime nature, no two leaves are the same shade of green. What a tremendous variety of nuances! If they are difficult to grasp by the reader, how much more difficult must it have been for the author to find and then to paint them.

Oh Richardson, I dare say that the truest of histories is filled with lies, whereas your novel is filled with truth. History depicts a few individuals: you depict all mankind; history imputes to certain individuals what they have not said or done; all that you attribute to man, he has said and done; history spans only one period in time, only one point on the earth's surface; you have encompassed all places and all ages. The human heart, which has been and will always be the same, is the model from which you copy. If one closely scrutinized the best historians, is there any one who would stand up to the test as well as you? Viewed from this angle, I dare say that history is often no more than a bad novel, while the novel, as you have written it, is good history. Oh painter of nature! it is you who never lies.

I will not cease to admire the tremendous mental prowess required of you to manipulate dramas of thirty or forty characters, each of whom conserves so rigorously the personality that you gave him; the profound knowledge of laws, customs, practices, morals, the human heart, and life; the inexhaustible wealth of morality, experience and observation which they require of you.

The interest and charm of the work conceal Richardson's art to those who are in the best position to perceive it. I began the reading of *Clarissa* several times in order to educate myself; so many times did I forget my aim on the twentieth page; like all the ordinary readers, I was struck only by the genius which there is to have imagined a young lady filled with wisdom and prudence, who does not take one step that is not false, but who is beyond accusation, since she had inhuman parents and an abominable man for a lover; to have given to this young prude the most vivid and the most frivolous of friends, who says and does nothing but the rational, but without any shock to her credibility; to have given to this friend a decent man for a lover, but one who is stuffy, ridiculous and chagrined by his mistress, in spite of the pleasantness and support of a mother who protects her; to have combined in this Lovelace the rarest of good qualities and the most hateful of vices, baseness with generosity, sincerity with frivolity, violence and control, good sense and madness; to have made of him a rogue who is hated, loved, admired, scorned, who stuns you in any of his forms, and who never maintains the same one for more than an instant. And this mass of secondary characters, how well portrayed they are! how many of them there are! This Belford with his friends, and Mrs. Howe and her Hickman, and Mrs. Norton, and the Harlowes—father, mother, brother, sisters, uncles and aunts— and all of the creatures who inhabit the place of debauchery! Such contrasts of motives and dispositions! how they all act and speak! How could a young lady alone against so many adversaries assembled, how could she not have succumbed! And then, such a fall!

Do people not recognize within such a diverse framework the same variety of characters, the same power of events and behavior in *Grandison*?

Pamela is a simpler work, less extensive, less complex; but is there any less genius in it? Now then, these three works, one of which would have sufficed to immortalize him, were done by one single man.

Since I have know them, they have become my touchstone; those who are displeased by them are judged for me. I have never spoken to a man that I respect without trembling at the idea that his opinion might not conform to mine. I have never met anyone who shared my enthusiasm, without being tempted to take him in my arms and embrace him.

Richardson lives no more. What a loss for letters and for humanity! This loss had affected me as if he were my brother. I carried him in my heart without ever having seen him, without knowing him other than through his works.

I have never met one of his fellow countrymen, or one of my own who had traveled in England, without asking: "Did you

see the poet Richardson?" And then, "Did you see the philosopher Hume?"

One day, a woman of taste and exceptional sensitivity who
was most preoccupied with the story of Grandison that she had
just read, said to a friend who was embarking for London:
"Would you please see Miss Emily, Mr. Belford and especially
Miss Howe for me, if she is still living."

Another time, a woman of my acquaintance who became involved in an exchange of letters which she believed to be innocent, became frightened at the fate of Clarissa, broke off this exchange at the very beginning of her reading of this work.

Have two friends ever argued, without my means of reconciling them having any success, because the one loathed Clarissa's
story, and the other worshipped it!

"Clarissa's piety annoys her!" Well then! Would she prefer
that an eighteen year-old girl, raised by virtuous Christian parents, timid, unfortunate in this life, with scarcely any more hope
of improving her lot except in another life, be without faith and
religion? This feeling is so great, so sweet, so touching in her;
her ideas of religion are so sound and pure; this sentiment gives
to her character such a pathetic nuance! No, no, you shall never
persuade me that this manner of thought is that of a dignified
person.

"She laughs when she sees this child become desperate because of her father's curse!" She laughs, and she is the mother of
children. I say to you that this woman can never be my friend.
You will see that the malediction of a respected father, a malediction which seems to have been put into force in several important places, should not be a terrible thing for a child of this
disposition! And who can say if in eternity God will not endorse
the sentence handed down by her father?

"She thinks it exaggerated that this reading makes me shed
tears!" And what always surprises me, when I am at the last
moments of this innocent girl, is that the stones, the walls, the
insensitive and cold blocks on which I tread are not touched
and do not unite their lament to mine. Then everything becomes
dark around me; my soul is filled with shadows; and it seems as

though nature covers itself with a heavy shroud.

"In her opinion, Clarissa's wit is made of composing sentences, and when she has done a few of them, she is then consoled." I confess to you that it is a great curse to feel and to think like that; so great in fact that I would prefer that my own daughter would die in my arms than to know that she was stricken. My own daughter! . . . Yes, I have thought about it, and I have not changed my mind.

"Continue to work, oh great man, work and exhaust yourself: see the approach of the end of your career at a time when others are beginning their own, so that similar judgements may be brought to your masterpieces! Nature, take centuries to prepare a man such as Richardson; wear yourself out in order to endow him; be ungrateful toward your other children, it will be for only a small number of souls such as mine that you will have engendered; and the tear which will fall from my eyes will be the unique reward of its vigils."

And in a postscript, she adds: "You ask me for the burial and the last will and testament of Clarissa, and I am sending them to you; but I would never forgive you as long as I live for having shared them with this woman. I retract that: read those two passages to her yourself, and do not fail to tell me that her laughs accompanied Clarissa to her final resting place, so that my aversion for her will be complete."

In matters of taste, just as in matters concerning religion, there is, as can be seen, a type of intolerance which I blame, but which I could not be sure of except through the application of my reason.

I was with a friend when I was handed the scene of Clarissa's burial and testament, two passages that the French translator omitted, without anyone really knowing why. This friend is one of the most sensitive men I know, and one of Richardson's most ardent worshippers, almost as fanatical as myself. He grabbed the books and withdrew to a corner and read. I observed him: at first I saw tears flow, he stopped, he sobbed; all of a sudden he rose, he walked without knowing where, he let out the cries of a desolate man, and directed the most bitter reproaches against the entire Harlowe family.

I had made the intention to note the beautiful passages of Richardson's three poems; but by what means? There are so many of them!

I only recall that the one hundred and twenty-eighth letter, from Mrs. Harvey to her niece, is a masterpiece; without affectation, without apparent skill, with a basis of truth that is inconceivable, she removes from Clarissa all hope of reconciliation with her parents, promotes the views of her ravisher, delivers her to his wickedness, resolves her to the trip to London, to listen to proposals of marriage, etc. I do not know what she is not capable of; she accuses the family while apologizing for them, she points out the need for Clarissa's flight, while denouncing it. This is one of many places where I cried: "Divine Richardson!" But in order to experience this emotion, one must begin the work and read up to this point.

In my copy I marked the one hundred and twenty-fourth letter, from Lovelace to his accomplice Leman, as a charming passage: there one can see all of the folly, the mirth, the treachery and the wit of this character. We do not know if this devil should be loved or detested. How he seduces that poor servant! The *good*, the *honest Leman*. How he represents the reward which awaits him! "You will be the proprietor of the White Bear Inn; your wife will be called madam hostess," and then in conclusion, "I am your friend Lovelace." Lovelace does not stop at minor formalities, when it is a matter of his success: all those who concur with his views are his friends.

There was only one great master who could conceive of associating with Lovelace this troop of men fallen from honor and corrupted, these vile creatures who irritate him with mockeries and who harden him in crime. If Belford stands up alone against his wretched friend, how inferior he is to him! What great genius was needed to introduce and maintain some balance between so many conflicting interests!

And do people believe that it was unintentional that the author imparted to his hero that warmth of imagination, that horror of marriage, that unbridled taste for intrigue and liberty, that limitless vanity, so many good qualities and vices.

Poets, learn from Richardson how to give confidants to the

wicked, so as to reduce the monstrosity of their crimes by dispersing them; and, in the opposite vein, to impart none of it to worthy people, so as to allow them the full worth of their goodness.

With what skill this Lovelace degrades and elevates himself! Study the one hundred and seventy-fifth letter. These are the sentiments of a cannibal; it is the cry of a savage beast. Four lines of postscript transform him suddenly into a good man or very close to it.

Grandison and *Pamela* are two fine works also, but I prefer *Clarissa* to them. Here the author does not take one step that is not a stroke of genius.

However, one does not see the arrival at the door of his lordship the father of Pamela, who had walked the entire night; one does not hear him talking to the house servants, without experiencing the most violent shudders.

The entire episode of Clementine in *Grandison* is one of the greatest beauty.

And what is the moment when Clementine and Clarissa become two sublime creatures? The moment when one loses her honor and the other her senses.

I never remember without trembling Clementine's entrance to her mother's chamber, pale, distraught eyes, her arm wrapped in a bandage, her blood flowing down her arm and dripping from the tips of her fingers, and her words: "Look, mother, it is your own." That tears the heart in two.

But why is Clementine interesting in her madness? It is that since she no longer controls her thoughts and mind, or the movements of her heart, if some shameful thing occurred inside her, she would escape from it. But she says no word which is without candor and innocence; and her condition does not permit us to doubt what she says.

It has been said to me that Richardson had spent several years in society, almost without saying a word.

He has not had all of the acclaim which he deserves. What passion is that of envy! It is the most cruel of the Furies: it follows a man of reputation to the edge of his grave; there, it disappears, and the justice of time sits in its place.

Oh Richardson! if in your lifetime you did not enjoy all of the renown which you deserved, how great you will be among your descendents, when they see you from as far away as we see Homer! Then who would dare to remove a single line from your sublime work? You have had more admirers here among us than you did in your own country; and that delights me. Oh centuries, hurry down to us with the honors which are due to Richardson! I call upon all those now listening to be my witnesses; I have never waited for someone else to pay homage to you before I did; from this day I kneel in front of your statue; I worshipped you, searching in the depths of my soul for the words to fully convey the admiration I have for you, and I did not find them. You who scan the lines I have just traced so haphazardly, unpreparedly and disjointedly, to the degree that they were inspired in the chaos of my heart, if heaven has granted you a more sensitive soul than my own, then erase them. Richardson's genius has eradicated whatever I had. His ghosts roam about without cease in my imagination; if I want to write, I hear Clementine's plea; Clarissa's shadow appears before me; I see Grandison walking before me; Lovelace upsets me, and the pen falls from my fingers. And you, more sweet specters, Emily, Charlotte, Pamela, dear Miss Howe, while I talk with you, the years of work and the winning of laurels pass by; and I approach the final stage, without attempting anything which could recommend me to future generations.

VIII
LACLOS: MODERN APPROACHES
TO THE FRENCH NOVEL

Pierre Ambroise Choderlos de Laclos (1741-1803) was an unlikely novelist. The majority of his active life was devoted to a military career, and an illustrious one. Laclos was an artillery specialist who was promoted regularly through the ranks to the grade of general. In spite of his initial political preferences for the Duc d'Orléans, he survived the tempests of the French Revolution with only temporary difficulties. In 1793, he conducted experiments on the hollow exploding shell which revolutionized artillery warfare.

Laclos is known today for only one novel, *Les Liaisons dangereuses* (1782).[1] This single work truly fulfilled the author's aspirations expressed prior to its publication:

> I was stationed on the Isle of Ré, and, after writing several insignificant funeral eulogies, a few epistles in verse, most of which will never be printed, luckily for me and for the public, after studying a trade which was not to bring me any major advancement or respect, I decided to write a work which would be a departure from the routine path, a work which would make a stir, and which would still be echoing on the earth long after I had left it.[2]

Indeed, *Les Liaisons dangereuses* attained a degree of perfection in style, technique and form that was unprecedented in eighteenth-century France. Laclos seemed to have studied the shortcomings of his predecessors in the novel and profited from their weaknesses. His modernism is also apparent in his critical ideas. He replaced the old fictional values of the seventeenth-century romances with standards properly suited to his time. Although he contributed only one masterpiece to French fiction, Laclos was a serious literary critic. His review of Fanny Burney's novel *Cecilia* in 1784 contains his most explicit ideas on the novel, and will be discussed in detail (see Appendix I). Laclos was also a philosopher of sorts, and expressed some quite modernistic ideas on the plight and potential of woman in his treatise of 1785, *De L'Education des femmes.* This text also provides information concerning the author's notion of the proper aims of literature. Like the majority of French novelists of the eighteenth century, Laclos wrote prefatory texts for his novel, an "Avertissement" and a "Préface du rédacteur." But these documents are quite inharmonious with the author's serious opinions found in the other discussions of the novel; as Baudelaire observed, "Editor's Forward and Author's Preface: artificial and concealed sentiments."[3] Finally, Laclos exchanged eight letters with Madame Riccoboni after the publication of *Les Liaisons dangereuses;* some of these letters have import as to the subject of the novel, and will also be examined (see Appendix II).

In his review of Fanny Burney's *Cecilia,* Laclos wrote a detailed commentary on that novel, as well as a scholarly introduction to the genre. The first paragraph of the review is of particular interest:

> Of all the genres produced by literature, there are few of lesser esteem than that of novels; but there is none that is more universally sought after or more avidly read. This contradiction between public opinion and behavior has often been pointed out; but the blissful unconcern of readers has not been bothered. Most men would abandon even their pleasures, if they had to go to the trouble of reflecting on them (Appendix I, first paragraph).

This observation is striking in its accuracy and scope. Prior to Laclos, the fundamental paradox of the French novel was that it was practiced by the best writers, and denounced by them almost at the same time. It was indeed the most frequently selected and most popular literary genre in progress then, yet the hypocrisy between theory and practice continued. This paragraph is consequently an astute identification of the "dilemma" of the French novel prior to 1784.

The reasons Laclos provided for this contradiction can be easily surmised from preceding criticism of the genre by French authors; it was considered very easy by comparison to the structural exigencies of the other neo-classical genres, and it was viewed as morally corrupt. Yet like Crébillon *fils,* Laclos was an optimist in matters concerning the novel, and professed that he did not concur with general opinions. Unlike other French novelists and critics, Laclos broke completely with old literary values which had enshrined the epic, history and the drama, and excluded the novel. His point of view was the opposite; these established genres were the subordinates, not the novel: "History teaches the morals of a nation, but not of its citizens. . . history tells of a few effects, and carefully conceals the causes . . .everything cannot be represented in the theater. All personalities are not appropriate here, and the ones that do appear. . . cannot be developed to their full extent" (Appendix I).

Thus the lengthy efforts by novelists and critics to hide the illegitimate novel behind a more legitimate one (Prévost in the case of history, Crébillon *fils* and Diderot to a lesser extent, in the case of the drama) have been discarded and even reversed. Those qualities which had normally been considered as artistic and superior (dramatic concision and limitation, historical authenticity), are viewed here as weaknesses when compared to the vast potential of the novel. To paraphrase Laclos' own words, the dramatist has to abandon all that is not absolutely essential, while the novelist is entitled to use any material which is not absolutely superfluous. The ideological progress found here represents a literary revolution since the time of Boileau.

Another striking innovation in Laclos' approach to the novel is found in the remaining paragraphs of the review, in which he provides a series of rules for the creation of prose fiction. The primary purpose of the novel is "a more profound knowledge of man's heart and mind, and this knowledge does not seem to us as being easy to acquire." The function of the novel is to depict "the full force of truth, whereas in the theater, one is almost always compelled to subdue its expression." Thirdly, the novelist must be morally useful, and here Laclos agrees with other theoreticians. Finally, the three principal requirements for novelists are to "observe, feel, and portray."

Laclos is thus the most specific of the eighteenth-century novelists, in terms of criteria. His introduction to *Cecilia* is more sweeping and less subjective than Diderot's *Eloge de Richardson,* and not limited to one particular author. The first two rules serve to reiterate the amplitude of the novel as a means of surpassing other genres in the search for a complete *tableau de la vie humaine.* Other novelists merely mentioned that ideal; Laclos appears to be the first to have believed it. The progress achieved since Montesquieu's definition of novelists as "a type of poet who shock both the language of the mind and that of the heart," and "who spend their lives in search of nature but never find it," is considerable.

Laclos projected his theoretical belief in the novel's superiority onto another level. In *De L'Education des femmes,* he further defined the relationship between fiction and morality. He identified reading as a logical and essential supplement to a woman's physical education and social training. He also recommended the works which involves morals, history and letters: they are travel literature, novels and dramas.[4]

Although he saw some potential danger in literary texts, Laclos' curriculum of education for women was more progressive than Rousseau's; the latter had remarked in his preface to *La Nouvelle Héloïse* that chaste girls never read any novels; in *L'Emile,* the male pupil was permitted to read only one novel, *Robinson Crusoe.* For Laclos, fiction had educational merit because it provided a more immediate and more realistic model to imitate, one which was more relevant for young people than the lessons from antiquity or the abstract rules of the *moralistes.*

The education of La Marquise de Merteuil in *Les Liaisons dangereuses* bears directly on Laclos' theory of education. Letter LXXXI of the work is another educational treatise: "I studied our morals in novels; our attitudes among the philosophers; I even searched in the works of the strictest moralists what they expected of us." The problem was that La Merteuil transformed those principles to a use that was contrary to their original intent:

> And I thus assured myself of what could be done, of how one should think, and how one had to appear. Once these three objects were established, only the last one posed any problems in its execution; I hoped to conquer them, and I began contemplating the means (*O. C.,* p. 203).

La Merteuil did not read only for self-improvement then, but to find the means of manipulating others to her own advantage. Her ironic treatment of educational material is further emphasized in Letter XXIX of the novel, where Cécile Volanges unwittingly falls under the same corrupted program of La Merteuil.

Laclos had distinct preferences among novelists. He was in a position to review the works of the preceding part of the eighteenth century, and these preferences were directed—logically enough—toward the epistolary novel. His debt to Rousseau is seen from the title-page of *Les Liaisons dangereuses*, on which the arrogant first sentence of *La Nouvelle Héloïse* is found verbatim. Laclos also adopted Rousseau's point of view in his own text: he claimed to be merely the *rédacteur* of his letters. In the last paragraph of his review of *Cecilia*, he stated:

> Finally, we feel that this novel should be included with the best works of this genre, nonetheless excluding *Clarissa*, the novel which demonstrated the greatest genius; *Tom Jones*, the best structured novel, and *La Nouvelle Héloïse*, the most beautiful work produced under the title of novel.

Clarissa Harlowe and *La Nouvelle Héloïse* were precisely the two most successful European novels of the eighteenth century. Laclos' respect for them deserves a qualification, however, since Rousseau considered his work as anything but a novel.

Laclos' esteem for Rousseau is reiterated elsewhere in *Les Liaisons dangereuses*. In Letter X, La Merteuil quoted *La Nouvelle Héloïse* as well as Crébillon's *Sopha* and La Fontaine's *contes*, in the interest of finding a tone and an expression suitable for the seduction of her "chevalier." Later, in Letter XXXIII, she placed Rousseau's work above all others as a model of style in the novel. Laclos' clearest expression of homage to Rousseau is found in a letter written to his wife during his incarceration:

> So you think that Rousseau and I write similarly. You are surely paying me a great honor, and are misleading yourself; but he wrote almost everything you have inspired and continue to inspire in me, and you mistake the similarity of the feeling for that of the expression. However, talent

> aside, I assure you that I know of no one but him who is
> capable of being the interpreter of my feelings for you,
> and perhaps he and I were the only ones capable of
> speaking a language which is suited to your heart, one that
> you can understand and appreciate as well.[5]

Without entering into a detailed evaluation of Laclos' merits versus those of Rousseau, we can still observe that for the author of *Les Liaisons dangereuses,* Rousseau was the unrivaled master of sentiment. *La Nouvelle Héloïse* was the manual of love in the eighteenth-century novel, and it comes as no surprise that Mme de Laclos had read it and compared her husband's style to it.

As seen in Laclos' review of *Cecilia,* Samuel Richardson's *Clarissa* ranked very close to *La Nouvelle Héloïse* in Laclos' list of masterful novels. In *De L'Education des femmes,* Laclos, like Diderot, exalted the misfortunes of Richardson's heroine as an exemplum of virtue:

> But if, on the other hand, it is pointed out to the young
> person that Clarissa, endowed with all of the natural ad-
> vantages and all virtues, allowed herself one single action
> against her parents' will, an action that she may have con-
> sidered to be innocent or even justified, if it is pointed
> out that from this moment she is irrevocably drawn into
> all of the misdeeds and becomes their victim, then there
> are few readings which could be more useful (*O. C.,* p.
> 479).

Coincidentally, Valmont's footman and personal spy, Azolan, reported to his master that La Tourvel was reading a volume of *Pensées Chrétiennes* and the first part of *Clarissa* (Letter CVII). These two works were not arbitrarily chosen by Laclos; they in fact reveal the polarized existence of La Tourvel, who on the one hand adhered to virtuous principles, and succumbed to Valmont on the other.

Just as he had confronted the esthetic dilemma of the French novel, Laclos also attempted to solve its problem of immorality. While the vast majority of French authors adver-tised the moral value of their works, few were taken seriously. As seen in his review of Fanny Burney, Laclos did not concur with the idea that classical genres were necessarily useful for moral instruction. His most explicit discussion of moral benefit in the novel is found in a series of letters exchanged with Madame Riccoboni after the publication of *Les Liaisons dangereuses.* Madame Riccoboni initiated the exchange in April, 1784, by complimenting Laclos on his excellent style and the fame he had achieved. But she accused him of not having fulfilled the double role of a good writer, that of moral utility as well as entertainment (*O. C.,* p. 711). She also chided him for presenting France in a very unfavorable light, and for portraying La Merteuil *too favorably,* to the detriment of good women.

The fourth letter of this correspondence (Appendix II) contains Laclos' self-defense. He insisted that he was not a misogynist, as implied by his accuser. And his means of defense is interesting: he justified his characterization of La Merteuil by reference to Molière's portrayal of Tartuffe. According to him, both characters possessed more vice than could ever be found in any one living being. For Madame Riccoboni, *Tartuffe* was an acceptable example of vice punished, because civil justice triumphed in the end. Laclos' rebuttal was even more perspicacious:

> I will permit myself in turn to make an observation of what you said to me concerning this play; it is that Tartuffe is not at all punished by laws, but by authority. I make this remark because it appears to me that the right of the moralist, whether he be a dramatist or a novelist, begins only where the laws cease. Molière himself seems to be of this opinion, so much so that he took care to protect from attack against the law even things such as the illegal gift of Orgon to Tartuffe. In effect, once men are assembled in society, they have the right to make their own laws only in cases of crimes which the government is not responsible for punishing. This public justice consists of ridicule for character flaws and indignation for vices. Tartuffe's punishment is in itself a continuation of the indignation of the monarch; and the punishment is provoked by other actions than those which occur during the course of the play (*O. C.,* pp. 720-721).

Laclos' choice of supporting evidence from the classical comedy differs from the approach used by Crébillon *fils* in the Preface to *Les Egarements du coeur et de l'esprit.* Molière had assumed the right to shock the public, in order to reform it. Laclos, reserving the same right as a moralist, "whether he be a dramatist or a novelist," merely cites a literary precedent. Here the novel, like the comedy, is seen as being quite capable of filling in gaps left by the law. The reservations of Crébillon *fils* and Prévost concerning this capability of the novel have been replaced by a prescription for social responsibility. Laclos did of course execute this theoretical belief in practice: La Merteuil is severely punished at the end of *Les Liaisons dangereuses,* by smallpox and even the loss of an eye, and also by the ridicule from her acquaintances. Whereas the legal system punished her in the form of financial ruin, it was transcended by the public's indignation.

It is impossible to account for the excellence of written style of Laclos' novel in a few short lines. It should at least be noted, however. Variation of style in a letter novel is a difficult task, but one which is necessary for the narrative form selected. The reader has only to examine the first few letters of this novel to become aware of the differences of expression of Cécile, who has just left the convent, and who writes like a naïve girl, of La Merteuil, who resembles a general ordering her troops into position, and Valmont, also a conqueror who talks in terms of missions, enemies, glory, and so on. A master ironist, Valmont acquiesces to La Merteuil's imperial orders, without revealing where his true intentions reside.

As was mentioned above, La Merteuil was considerably well-read and educated; she is the spokesman for Laclos in matters of language and style. In Letter CV of the novel, she attempts to teach Cécile that proper expression is one of the laws of their world; in Letter XX, she cautioned Valmont that in serious affairs, the only acceptable proofs are written ones. This observation is important because La Merteuil's letters were one of the causes of her own destruction.[6]

The other young victim, Danceny, realized too late the importance of letters in the sinister world of Valmont and La Merteuil:

> But a letter is the portrait of the soul. Unlike a cold image, it does not have that stagnancy so far removed from love; it follows our every movement; turn by turn

it becomes animated, it delights, then it rests (Letter CL).

Laclos exploited another aspect of the epistolary novel, that is, the multiplicity of viewpoints on a given situation, or the "chamber of mirrors" effect. A notable example is the scene of Valmont's seduction of Cécile: in Letter XCVI, Valmont narrates the actual seduction to La Merteuil; in the following letter (XCVII), Cécile provides her own account of the seduction, and conveys her state of emotional disarray. Finally, in the next letter, Madame Volanges writes to La Merteuil that some misfortune has happened to her daughter, but she is not sure what precisely did happen. La Merteuil was of course fully informed, and each letter reveals the amount of intelligence granted to the various correspondents, with the reader enjoying the most advantageous perspective.

Laclos was so far removed from the system of esthetic values of preceding French novelists that he was able to parody their older values. In *Les Liaisons dangereuses,* characters are divided into two groups: the predators (Valmont and La Merteuil) and their victims (Cécile, Danceny and La Tourvel). The victims are treated by the stronger figures as if they were fictional characters, not real persons. Cécile is introduced by La Merteuil to Valmont as "the heroine of this new novel" (Letter II); Danceny is referred to as a "Céladon," the hero of D'Urfé's pastoral romance *L'Astrée* (Letter LI), and as "that handsome hero of a novel" (LXIII). Above all, La Tourvel, the ultimate victim, is the main character of this novel within the larger novel: Valmont reveals his plan in Letter CX to make her a "new Clarissa." *Les Liaisons dangereuses* was so far advanced from the *roman précieux,* the main point of reference for the novel in the first part of the eighteenth century, that Laclos was able to parody it by the means of his characters.[7]

But Laclos was not totally detached from the seventeenth century; as was seen, he found support for the moral function of the novel in Molière's comedy. His own novel is also classical, in the sense of clarity, the use of dramatic irony, and mastery of style.

Les Liaisons dangereuses was the culminating point in the development of art in the French novel of the Enlightenment, and more specifically, the epistolary novel. It is the harem

intrigue of *Les Lettres persanes* exploited to full length. It presents all of the diversifications of points of view in the letter
novel, as opposed to the *monodie épistolaire* found in Crébillon
fils. *Les Liaisons dangereuses* is everything that *La Nouvelle
Héloïse* could have been, if it had been purified of its disserta-
tions and digressions.

Laclos wrote a novel because he believed in the merits inherent in the genre. He went so far as to recommend it as one
element of a serious program of education. His praise of the
masterpieces of Fielding, Richardson and Rousseau is far more
consistent with the reality of the novel's situation than are the
condemnations of the others. His art in the novel rendered the
confusion over the idea of *le roman* an anachronism.

NOTES

[1]All of my translations and references to Laclos' works are based on Maurice Allem's preparation of Laclos' *OEuvres complètes* in the Bibliothèque de la Pléiade (Paris: Gallimard, 1951), referred to as *O. C.*

[2]This is Alexandre de Tilly's quotation of Laclos, in *O. C.*, p. 732. Tilly's accuracy is often questioned because of his excessive admiration for Laclos. See Laurent Versini, *Laclos et la tradition: Essai sur les sources et la technique des Liaisons dangereuses* (Paris: Klincksieck, 1968), pp. 26-30.

[3]"Notes de Charles Baudelaire sur *Les Liaisons dangereuses*," in *O. C.*, p. 738. Although some modern critics (Versini, Allem, Thelander) accept the two prefaces to Laclos' novel as being authentic, I agree with Baudelaire in that the two documents are atypical of Laclos' ideas expressed elsewhere.

[4]*O. C.*, p. 475.

[5]Translated from *Lettres inédites de Choderlos de Laclos,* ed. by Louis de Chauvigny (Paris: Société du Mercure de France, 1904), p. 60.

[6]Philip Thody, *Les Liaisons dangereuses* (London: Camelot Press, 1970), p. 29.

[7]For a detailed discussion of this parody of the *roman précieux* within Laclos' text, see my essay "Laclos and Standards in Fiction," in *Kentucky Romance Quarterly* (1978).

LACLOS: APPENDIX I
"SUR LE ROMAN DE: *CECILIA*" (1784)

Of all the genres produced by literature, there are few of lesser esteem than that of novels; but there is none that is more universally sought after or more avidly read. This contradiction between public opinion and behavior has often been pointed out; but the blissful unconcern of the readers has not been bothered. Most men would abandon even their pleasures if they had to go to the trouble of reflecting on them.

Thus it has been generally agreed to attach little importance to novels. Some people have said this, because it is what they thought; the majority of people have thought the same, because a few had said it, and the judgment stood. The reasons that are given are, on the one hand, the ease of the genre, and on the other, its inutility. We declare that we do not agree. Indeed, how can one imagine the ease of a genre whose success is so rare? How can we deem worthless works which teach us the most important things to learn? Such, however, are novels.

If we except the epic poem, in which French literature has been especially impoverished, no other genre, not even the theater, has yielded proportionately as many works which have fallen into oblivion; and we must also observe that even among the former group, some of them offer random portions or even entire parts which would have lent dignity to any other production. But the supposed freedom enjoyed by the novelist constantly provokes the criticism of the reader, who appears to permit nothing but the right to expect everything. What is then this claimed freedom from all rules which is presented as such a great advantage? Is it not necessary for novels, like any other work, to entertain, instruct and be interesting? And since no path has been prescribed to arrive at this fundamental goal, will it be concluded that it is easier not to deviate? We are inclined to believe, however, that few works require a more profound knowledge of man's heart and mind, and this knowledge does not seem to us as being easy to acquire. Surely, it alone can constitute the merit of a novel, and when it is present in them, we feel that the work becomes pleasant and useful at the same time. This last remark will not pass without objection, but tell us then where else one can learn to know morals, characters, sentiments and passions.

History teaches us the morals of a nation, but not of its citizens; it relates public morals, and suppresses private ones; it depicts men as they depict themselves, and not as they are. Individual memoirs portray individuals only, and are incapable of choosing anyone but those who were exceptional. As for sentiments and passions, history tells of a few effects, and carefully conceals the causes. We add that the enlightenment which it spreads, which is always aimed at sovereigns, never shows us their peoples except in their relations with those who lead them.

The theater offers surely portraits which are truer and closer to society; but everything cannot be represented in the theater. All personalities are not appropriate here, and the ones that do appear, and most favorably so, cannot be developed to their full extent. It is the same with sentiments and passions; let us at least understand that one of the principles which distinguish the skill of a dramatic author from that of a novelist, is that the one considers superfluous everything which is not necessary, whereas the other must select as being useful all which is not superfluous. There remains to point out that one can, that one even should give to the portrayals presented in a novel the full force of the truth, whereas in the theater, one is almost always compelled to subdue its expression. This requirement, very little understood in our time, is a natural consequence of the difference between dramatized action and narrated action. It then ensues that in the theater, the most favorably depicted character leaves a vast area for expansion by the novelist. Molière had portrayed Tartuffe when Marivaux portrayed his Monsieur de Climal, and neither of these portraits harmed the other.

If someone suspected us of wanting to associate Marivaux with Molière, we would reply. . . No, on second thought, there would be no reply. What would we have to say to the person who conceived such a strange notion? But let us continue.

If history and the theater can provide us with nothing more than an incomplete knowledge of man, we must then look for it in works by the moralists; but since novels are usually excluded from this category, some of them have proven that it was the fault of the author alone, and not that of genius; and those are the ones that deserve our attention. Considered from this point of view, novels are entitled to our forgiveness—better yet—to the public's respect, for the good which they can accomplish, and for the talent which they require.

To observe, feel and portray, these are the three qualities necessary to an author of novels. May he possess both finesse and profundity, tact and delicacy, grace and truth; but may he above all possess that precious sensitivity without which there is no talent, and which alone can replace all the others. . . .

[The remaining portion of Laclos' review is devoted exclusively to Fanny Burney's novel, and contributes little else to his own system of artistic criteria. The review is quite complimentary, as indicated in the last few lines, provided below.]

Finally, we feel that this novel should be included with the best works of this genre, nonetheless excluding *Clarissa,* the novel which demonstrates the greatest genius; *Tom Jones,* the best structured novel, and *La Nouvelle Héloïse,* the most beautiful work produced under the title of novel.

LACLOS: APPENDIX II
LETTER TO MME RICCOBONI (1784)

It is I again, Madam, and I fear that you might find me a nuisance; but how could I not respond to your obliging letter! How could I not return your expression of thanks? What can I say? This correspondence may cease, and I expect it to; I know you have the right to fall silent, and I would have no means to object to it; but you surely do not expect me to be the one to initiate it. A long time ago I learned to deprive myself, but not to do so unnecessarily.

No, Madam, I did not at all suspect you of having an author's prejudice; who could inspire such a thing in you? What could be written that would destroy the charm of those delightful works which you name trivial, but which will always be cherished, as long as we value noble and delicately expressed sentiments. But, you say, you are a woman and a Frenchwoman! Well, I am not frightened by either of those two qualities; I feel that I hold inside me enough strength so as to not fear such a tribunal.

Perhaps these same *Liaisons dangereuses,* so criticized by women today, are a rather significant proof that I am deeply concerned with women; how can one be concerned with them and not love them?

If I have seen some women, repudiated by their sex due to depravities and wickedness, if I was struck by their evil or by the evil which they might do, I sounded the alarm and exposed their corrupt ruses, and rendered nothing but a good service to honest women; how then could I be reproached for having struggled against the enemy who shamed them and could harm them?

But, it continues, you create monsters to combat them; such women do not exist. Let us allow for that possibility, I agree;

why, then, is there so much ado? When Don Quixote took up arms to go and combat the windmills, did anyone undertake to defend them? We pitied him, but we did not incriminate him. Let us return to the truth.

People press me and interrogate me: did a Madame de Merteuil ever exist? I do not know. I did not attempt to libel anyone, but when Molière portrayed Tartuffe, was there any man who, under the cloak of religion, undertook to seduce the mother of the girl he was to marry, divide the father and son, rob the former of his fortune and finish by becoming the victim's informer in the effort of escaping his accusations? No, surely not, this man never lived; but twenty or even a hundred hypocrites had individually committed such horrors; Molière concentrated them on one hypocrite alone and delivered him to the indignation of the public.

You will certainly not suspect me of wanting to compare myself to Molière; but like him, I was able to combine in one figure the diverse traits of the same character. I did, therefore, portray or at least try to portray the ugliness which depraved women permit themselves, by covering their vices with moral hypocrisy.

If no woman ever gave herself over to debauchery while feigning devotion to love, if one has ever helped or even provoked the seduction of a friend, a *dear friend;* if no woman has ever felt the desire to destroy or who did in fact destroy her lover who had been too unfaithful; if there has never been seen someone in this wave of vile passions commit a major crime for a very small gain; finally, if this word *gaity* has not been indiscriminately defiled by men and women to express horrors which ought to shock every decent man; if all of that is not true, I was wrong to write. . .but who will dare deny the truth which is seen every day?

There, Madam, are some of the reasons which I repeated to myself before publishing my work and which I may one day have to reveal to all. There are still others, but is not to you that all of them need to be said.

I would like to add, however, that Mme de Merteuil is no more French than any other nationality. Anywhere that a woman is born with active senses and heart closed to love, with some wit and a vile soul, who is wicked and whose corruption would be penetrating but without energy, there would a Mme de Merteuil exist, under some varied disguise, and with merely local ornaments. If I gave a French appearance to her, it was that since I was convinced that the truth can be depicted only according to nature, I preferred the embellishments which I could find at hand, but the trained eye can easily penetrate the model and recognize the naked truth.

Madam, remain therefore a woman, and a Frenchwoman; cherish your sex and your country, both of which should be proud to have you; I will find some other reason to desire your patronage, but no other reason not to obtain it.

SADE: MORE RULES FOR THE NOVEL

The Marquis de Sade (1740-1814) requires very little introduction to the modern public. He is probably the most frequently cited French novelist of the eighteenth century. At the same time, he is often misunderstood: although he spent thirty years of his life in prison for sex-related crimes for the most part, citizen Sade contributed his services to the Revolutionary government in the area of hospital reform, and his additions to prose fiction remain significant.

Sade's *Reflections on the Novel* (*Idée sur les romans*)[1] is a curious document. Published in Year VIII of the Republic (1800) as a preface to *Les Crimes de l'amour*, the essay presents what Sade considered to be the origin of novels, followed by judgments on a large number of authors, and remarks on the esthetic and technical aspects of prose fiction.

In some cases, Sade's accounts of the works of other novelists are quite astute. Others are mildly appalling for their lack of depth or inaccuracy. For example, he identifies Mme de Lafayette as the outstanding French novelist of the seventeenth century, a choice which remains valid. On the other hand, he condemns Marivaux for a "precious and mannered style" (p. 105), i.e., that which constitutes Marivaux's uniqueness today. While admitting that Sade profited from historical hindsight more than the majority of other eighteenth-century writers, he nonetheless clarifies certain notions of the novel that were left unclarified by his predecessors; he recognizes hypocrisy in the theory of fiction, especially concerning the role of the novelist as a moralist, and he offers rules where there were no set rules.

Sade's approach to the very notion of *le roman* is more scientific than that of his predecessors, in that he begins his

essay with an etymological treatment of the very word.   The
term did indeed evolve from the vulgar Latin word *romanice*, as
attested in the survival of the word *romance*.   He demonstrates
his full awareness of the divorce between *le roman* and romance
by his association of the latter with "amorous adventures" (p.
98).

His historical approach is equally scientific.   After having
identified the point of origin of novels as being god-worshipping
countries, Sade traces the precedents of the novel from greco-
roman authors, through the Gallic bards, the *troubadours*, Italian
and Spanish contributors, and up to the first French "novelists"
of the seventeenth century.   Here also, Sade provides a modern
judgment, in the identification of *L'Astrée* and *La Princesse de
Clèves* as the pivotal points in the novel's development at that
time, but with most of his praise reserved for the brevity and
condensation of the latter text—qualities which account for its
greater interest.

Sade's moral points of view are also apparent in these early
pages of *Reflections on the Novel:* "Man is prey to two weaknesses, which derive from his existence and characterize it.   Wheresoever on earth he dwells, man feels the need to *pray,* and to
love: and herein lies the basis for all novels" (p. 99).   The relationship between these two areas, and the tendency among god-
worshipping peoples to foster fables, parables and ultimately
novels, is questionable.   As can be seen elsewhere in his *Reflections,* Sade does not always reason consistently.

As witnessed in the preceding treatment of French Enlightenment novelists, there was complete unanimity as to the
need for morality in the novel, at least the proclamation of such
a need.   The prefaces to *Manon Lescaut, Les Egarements du
coeur et de l'esprit* and *La Nouvelle Héloïse* contain the more
notable examples.   Laclos, who is often associated with Sade,
less for reasons of philosophical similarity than for chronological
proximity, felt a need to reiterate the moral purpose of the novel
as late as 1784:   "Is it not necessary for novels, like any other
work, to entertain, instruct and be interesting?" ("Sur le roman
de: *Cecilia*").

I will limit my discussion of the novelists mentioned by
Sade to those who appear in previous units in this work, although

this decision regrettably causes the omission of some interesting judgments on Restif de la Bretonne, for example, whom Sade loathed, and Voltaire, who is not generally classified as a novelist. He nonetheless identified cultural and social factors which accounted for the profound differences between the *romances* of the seventeenth century and the *novels* of the following one:

> The writers who emerged thereafter sensed that earlier insipidities would no longer amuse a century perverted by the Regency, a century which had recovered from the follies of chivalry, the absurdities of religion, and the adoration of woman, and which, finding it simpler to amuse or to corrupt these women than to serve them or shower fulsome praise upon them, created scenes, situations, and conversations more in keeping with the spirit of the times: they clothed cynicism and immorality in a pleasant, bantering, and sometimes even philosophical style, and at least gave pleasure if they did not edify (p. 105).

This indication of the change in attention by novelists is quite poignant and broad in scope, and will be treated further in the paragraphs below.

Sade's evaluation of Crébillon *fils* is most severe. In all three of Crébillons principal works—even *Les Egarements du coeur et de l'esprit*—he indulged in vice and strayed from virtue, according to Sade. Although he apparently was ignorant of *Les Lettres persanes,* Sade also criticized Marivaux for his *préciosité* and *maniérisme.* As one might expect, considerable praise is given to Rousseau, "to whom Nature had granted in refinement and sentiment what she had granted only in wit to Voltaire. . ." (p. 105). As might also be expected from the criticism of other authors, Fielding and Richardson ranked quite high in Sade's list of preferences:

> Finally, the English novels, the vigorous works of Richardson and Fielding, arrived to teach the French that 'tis not by portraying the fastidious languors of love or the tedious conversations of the bedchamber that one can obtain any success with the novel, but by depicting robust and manly characters who, playthings and victims of that effervescence of the heart known as love, reveal to us

both its dangers and its misfortunes; only by doing so
can this evolution be shown, this portrayal of passions so
carefully traced in the English novels (p. 106).

The notions of vigor as opposed to languor, and robustness as
opposed to tedium are judgmental and relative. But the very
authors indicated here by Sade had already admitted singular
preference for Richardson, at least. Sade's voice is merely one
more in support of that admiration.

Sade's treatment of Prévost is indicative of his own notion
of the novelist and the novel. He refers to Prévost first of all
as the "French Richardson,"[2] as the sole author who had "the
ability to hold the reader's attention for a long time," and as
having provided an idea of "what is called writing a novel" (pp.
107-108). In a footnote to his *Reflections*, Sade goes so far as
to call *Manon Lescaut* "our finest novel" (p. 108), and claims
that Rousseau's *Julie* would not have been possible without
Prévost's masterpiece.

This eulogy of Prévost points to the hypocrisy of French
novelists as moralists. *Manon Lescaut* deals precisely with a
"ruined girl," as Sade admits, and this factor sheds considerable
doubt on the claims of moral edification by the author. From
the models of the English novelists, he derived the principle
that " 'tis not always by making virtue triumph that a writer
arouses interest," and that this rule ". . .is simply one that we
should like all men to follow for our own sake and happiness,
and is in no wise essential in the novel, nor is't even the one
most likely to awaken the reader's interest" (p. 106). This refusal is formulated more succinctly several pages later: "Avoid
the affectation of moralizing: it has no place in the novel" (p.
112).

When compared with the evasiveness of his predecessors,
Sade's frankness is an asset. It is difficult to explain why authors
such as Prévost went to such length and difficulty in extolling
the moral profit found in his works, while very often surrounding
crime with "roses," as Sade accuses (p. 116). In *Le Dilemme du
roman au XVIIIe siècle*, Georges May presents several potential
explanations for this moralizing convention.[3] The first is the
argument of the *tableau de la vie humaine*, by which the novelists, in painting all aspects of society, reserved the right to

portray the evil members of society, as well as the good. May's second explanation is akin to the first: in the interest of this *tableau de la vie humaine,* the novelist adds to his abstract and impersonal moral doctrine the application of a concrete example. Finally, the remaining justifications of the claim of moral benefit follow logically from the first two: "la justice immanente," i.e., vice punished, and "le piège dénoncé," or the warning of evil to the unsuspecting.[4]

The tension between the theory of moral benefit and the actual texts is evident: it is difficult, if not impossible, to discuss the dangers of vice and crime, without directly discussing those very aspects. The most plausible explanation for the presence of *utile et dulci* in the eighteenth-century novel is that the promise of moral benefit, like the convention of authenticity, was another means of enhancing the prestige of a genre which lacked such prestige.

It is difficult to imagine the Marquis de Sade as a moralist. His *Philosophie dans le boudoir* surpasses the limits of the imagination in sexual brutality. *Les 120 Jours de Sodome* is basically a list of one bestiality after another. *Justine,* however, can be considered as an applied illustration of Sade's reversal of the virtue rewarded—vice punished tendency. Indeed, no attempt is made by the author to present virtue as receiving any reward. As Sade states in his *Reflections on the Novel,* the novelist's brush should portray man from within and seize him when he drops his mask (p. 110), and thus he avoids the problem of hypocrisy in the question of morality. It should also be mentioned in Sade's defense that he was capable of writing some rather conventional and coherent fiction. *Eugénie de Franval,* composed in 1788, is a unified and pleasant work; incest is one of the main preoccupations of the work, yet atrocities and graphic details are absent in it.

Sade's justification of his role as a moralist is based on his interpretation of nature, the same criterion invoked by Crébillon *fils,* Prévost and Laclos. And if we were to grant him the point of degree to which nature can be portrayed, his claim could be accepted:

> Unlike Crébillon and Dorat, I have not set myself the dangerous goal of enticing women to love characters who

> deceive them; on the contrary, I want them to loathe
> these characters. 'Tis the only way whereby one can
> avoid being duped by them. And, in order to succeed in
> that purpose, I painted that hero who treads the path of
> vice with features so frightful that they will most assured-
> ly not inspire either pity or love. In doing so, I dare say,
> I am become more moral than those who believe they
> have license to embellish them (pp. 115-116).

In this context, the *dulci* aspect of Horace's rule has been sacri-
ficed, ironic as it may seem, in favor of the *utile*. The "colors of
hell" are far more visible in Sade's work than those of heaven;
they are present to the point of depravity. There would apparently be a more subdued path to pursue, however, than the
extreme case found in Sade's works. He would have us believe
that he is simply being more faithful to nature than his fellow
writers.

In his introduction to *Reflections on the Novel,* Sade promised to confront the issue of rules for the genre. After having
eliminated the one which was most frequently cited by the other
novelists, he provided his own: 1) the most essential requirement
for the novelist's art is a knowledge of the human heart; 2) the
novelist is forbidden to stray from verisimilitude; 3) no barrier
should restrain the novelist; and 4) outbursts are desired from the
writer, and "flights of fancy" rather than adherence to rules (pp.
110-111).

Although these rules are slanted enough to be original, they
bear a striking similarity to Laclos' principles governing the
novel, as enumerated in his review of *Cecilia.* Laclos also speci-
fied verbatim a more profound knowledge of the human heart,
the imitation of nature, and the removal of restraints. Laclos was
also an advocate of lyricism or "flights of fancy," and, in view of
the strange silence by Sade regarding Laclos' work, the question
of the former's originality is posed.

Elsewhere in his *Reflections on the Novel,* Sade listed other
principles which were more modern and more original: work is
the surest source of the novelist's inspiration; secondary plots
should derive from and return to the main plot; it is essential that
local color be exact; and new material should be sought, not a
mere reworking of already oft-told tales (pp. 112-113). It is

recommendations such as these that one would expect to find in theoretical texts of other eighteenth-century authors, but which were merely implied in practice.

Sade is virtually unique in neoclassical fiction. He has forced the creation of special adjectives and terms for the analysis of his work. His uniqueness in the area of esthetics of the eighteenth-century French novel resides mainly in his candor. The Age of Reason was also an age of the cult of passion and the senses, with marked tendencies toward naturalism. Whereas passion had occupied the center stage of the novel before Sade, neoclassical rules required that it be subdued, if not absent. With the passing of neoclassicism, imitation also disappeared, and authors were no longer required to adhere to a theoretical code that had become ineffective in practice.

NOTES

[1]The translation of Sade's *Idées sur les romans* (*Reflections on the Novel*) used here is that of Austryn Wainhouse and Richard Seaver, in the *Marquis de Sade: The 120 Days of Sodom and Other Writings* (New York: Grove Press, 1966), reproduced with permission. My parenthetical references are to the pages of that edition.

[2]Sade also lauded Prévost for his translations of Richardson's novels. Subsequent research has indicated that Prévost's translations of Samuel Richardson were not as extensive as was previously believed.

[3]May, *Le Dilemme du roman au XVIIIe siècle*, chapter 4.

[4]*Ibid.*

SADE: APPENDIX
REFLECTIONS ON THE NOVEL (1800)

We give the name "novel" to any work of imagination fashioned from the most uncommon adventures which men experience in the course of their lives.

But why is this kind of literary work called a novel?[1]

Amongst what people did the novel originate, and what are the most famous examples that history has to offer?

And, finally, what are the rules one must follow in order to succeed in perfecting the art of writing the novel?

These are the three questions we propose to discuss.

Let us begin with the etymology of the word. There being no trace of this term, as it relates to this type of composition, amongst the peoples of antiquity, we must, it would seem to me, concentrate upon discovering how the term, which we still use today, first came into our language.

The "Romance" language was, as we know, a mixture of Celtic and Latin,[2] in use under the first two dynasties of our kings.[3] It is reasonable to assume that the works of the kind to which we are referring, written in this language, must have borne the same name, and the term *une romane* must have been used to describe a work in which the emphasis is upon amorous adventures, as the term *romance* was used to describe ballads or lays of the same type. All efforts to discover any other etymological origin for this word come to naught; as common sense offers no alternative, it would seem simplest to adopt the above.

Let us move on then to the second question.

Amongst what people did the novel originate, and what are the most famous examples history has to offer?

The novel is generally thought to have originated with the Greeks; from whom it passed over to the Moors and thence to the Spaniards, who subsequently transmitted it to our troubadours. And they in turn passed it on to our courtly storytellers.

Although I respect this theory of the novel's line of descent, and although there are even parts of it I subscribe to, I none the less can in no wise adopt it literally. Is it not, in fact, difficult to accept without reservation in an era when travel was so infrequent and communication so sporadic? There are customs, habits, and tastes which cannot be transmitted; inherent in all men, they are a part of man's make-up at birth. Wherever man exists, inevitable traces of these customs, habits, and tastes can be discovered.

Let there be no doubt about it: it was in the countries which first recognized gods that the novel originated; and, to be more specific, in Egypt, the cradle of all divine worship. No sooner did man begin to *suspect* the existence of immortal beings than he endowed them with both actions and words. Thereafter we find metamorphoses, fables, parables, and novels: in a word, we find works of fiction as soon as fiction seized hold of the minds of men. Thus we find fabulous works of imagination the moment it becomes a question of imaginary creatures: when whole nations, at first guide by priests, after having slaughtered each other in the name of their chimerical divinities, later take up arms for their king or their country, the homage offered to heroism counterbalances the tribute paid to superstition; not only do they then most rightly substitute these new heroes for their gods, but they also sing their warriors' praises as once they had sung the praises of heaven; they embroider upon the great feats of their lives, or, weary of relating tales about them, they create new characters who resemble them . . .who surpass them, and soon new novels appear, doubtless more probable and far more suitable for man than were those tales that extolled naught but phantoms. *Hercule*,[4] the mighty captain, having valiantly to do battle against his enemies: this is the historical hero; Hercules, destroying monsters, cleaving in twain giants: that is the god. . .the fable, and the origin of superstition; but of reasonable superstition, since its only basis is the reward for heroism, the gratitude due to the liberators of a nation, whereas the superstition that invents uncreated and never perceived beings has no other motive behind it than to provoke fear and hope, and to unsettle the mind.

Every people, therefore, has its gods, its demigods, its heroes, its true stories, and its fables; some part of it, as we have just seen, can have a solid basis in fact, as it pertains to the heroes; all the rest is pure fantasy, incredible; it is all a work of pure invention, a novel, because the gods spoke only through the medium of men who, more or less interested in this ridiculous artifice, did not fail to make up the language of phantoms, from whatever they imagined would be most likely to seduce or terrify, and, consequently, from whatever was most incredible. " 'Tis common knowledge," said the scholar Huet, "that the term 'novel' was once applied to history, and that it was later applied to fiction, all of which is proof positive that the one derived from the other."

There were, therefore, novels written in every language and in every country of the world, the events and styles of which were modeled both after the customs of the country and opinions commonly held therein.

Man is prey to two weaknesses, which derive from his existence and characterize it. Wheresoever on earth he dwells, man feels the need to *pray*, and to *love:* and herein lies the basis for all novels. Man has written novels in order to portray beings whom he *implored;* he has written novels to sing the praises of those whom he *loves.* The former, dictated by terror or hope, must have been somber, full of exaggeration, untruths, and fictions, such as those that Esdras composed during the Babylonian captivity. The latter are full of niceties and sentiments, as typified by Heliodorus' *Aethiopica*, a love story about Theagenes and Charicleia. But as man *prayed*, and as he *loved*, wheresoever he dwelled on the face of the earth, there were novels, that is, works of fiction, which at times depicted the fanciful objects of his worship, and at times those more concrete objects of his love.

One should therefore refrain from trying to trace the source of this kind of writing back to one nation in preference to another; one should be persuaded by what we have just said that all nations have more or less employed this form, depending upon the greater or lesser predilection they have had either for love or for superstition.

Let us cast a cursory glance now at those nations which have been most receptive to works of fiction, and at the works themselves and those who have written them. Let us follow the line down to our own day, in order to allow our readers to be in a position to make their own comparisons.

The earliest novelist whereof antiquity speaks is Aristeides of Miletus, but none of his work remains extant. All we know is that his prose romance was called *Milesian Tales*. A reference in the preface of *The Golden Ass* seems to indicate that Aristeides' works were licentious: "I am going to write in this same manner," says Apuleius, in the beginning of *The Golden Ass.*

Antonius Diogenes, a contemporary of Alexander, wrote in a more polished style in *The Loves of Dinias and Dercillis;* a novel full of fabrications, charms, and spells, of voyages, and of most remarkable adventures—a work that le Seurre copied in 1745, in a short, even more extraordinary work; for, not content to take his heroes through familiar lands, as had Diogenes, le Seurre at times takes them to the moon, and at times down into the bowels of hell.

Next come the loves of Rhodanes and Sinonis, written by Iamblichus of Syria; the loves of Theagenes and Charicleia which we have already mentioned; Xenophon's *Cyropaedia;* the loves of Daphnis and Chloë, by Longus; the loves of Ismene and Ismenia; and a whole host of others, some translated, others totally forgotten today.

The Romans, more critically minded and more given to spite and malice than to love and prayer, confined themselves to a few works of satire, such as those by Petronius and Varro, which should in no wise be classed as novels.

The Gauls, more inclined to these two weaknesses, had their bards, whom we can consider as the first novelists in that part of Europe wherein we dwell today. The occupation of these bards, says Lucan, was to render in verse the immortal acts of their nation's heroes, and to sing them to the accompaniment of an instrument which resembled a lyre; very few of these works have come down to us today.

Then we have the words and deeds of Charlemagne, attributed to Archbishop Turpin of Reims, and all the tales of the Round Table—Tristram, Lancelot, Perceval—all written with a view toward immortalizing known heroes or inventing others modeled after them but who, embellished by the imagination, surpass them by the wonderment of their deeds. But what a great gulf separates these long, boring, and superstition-laden works from the Greek novels which had preceded them! What barbarity, what coarseness followed after those tasteful and pleasing works of fiction whereof the Greeks had given us the models; for though there were doubtless others before them, these are the earliest with which we are familiar today.

The troubadours were next to appear, and although we ought to class them as poets rather than as novelists, the multitude of agreeable tales in prose that they composed is none the less reason enough for us to grant them a rightful place amongst the writers of whom we are speaking. Let anyone who doubts this claim cast his eyes upon their *fabliaux*—written in the Romance language during the reign of Hugh Capet[5]—which Italy hastened to emulate.

This beautiful part of Europe, still groaning beneath the yoke of the Saracens and still far removed in time from that period when she was to become the birthplace of the Renaissance in the arts, boasted almost no novelists prior to the tenth century. They appeared more or less at the same time as did our troubadours in France, and indeed imitated them. But let us be quite candid concerning this glory: it was not the Italians who became our masters in this art, as Laharpe contends (page 242, vol. III), but, on the contrary, on our own soil in France that they received their training: 'twas at the school of our troubadours that Dante, Boccaccio, Tasso, and even to some degree Petrarch, sketched out their compositions; almost all of Boccaccio's tales can be found as well in our own *fabliaux*.

The same cannot be said for the Spanish, versed in the art of fiction by the Moors, who themselves derived it from the Greeks, having the entire body of Greek fiction translated into Arabic;

they wrote delightful novels, much imitated by our writers; of which more later.

As gallantry took on a new aspect in France, the novel improved, and 'twas then, that is to say at the beginning of the previous century, that Honoré d'Urfé wrote his novel *Astrée,* which led us to prefer—and most deservedly so—his charming shepherds of the Lignon to those foolish knights of the eleventh and twelfth centuries. From that time forth, the rage to emulate seized all those whom Nature had endowed with a taste for this kind of writing. The astonishing success of *Astrée,* which was still being widely read midway through the present century, had completely captured people's fancies, and the work was widely imitated, though never improved upon. Gomberville, La Calprenède, Desmarets, and Scudéry all thought to surpass the original by substituting princes and kings for the Lignon shepherds, and they slipped back into the error which their model had managed to avoid. Scudéry's sister made the same mistake as her brother: like him, she wanted to ennoble d'Urfé's manner and style and, like her brother, she substituted boring heroes for charming shepherds. Instead of portraying, in the person of Cinna, a prince such as Herodotus had painted him, she composes an Artamène more insane than all the characters in *Astrée,* a lover who can do naught but weep from morn till night, and whose languors, instead of becoming an object of interest to us, only tax our patience. The same drawbacks in her *Clélie,* wherein she endows the Romans, whom she badly distorts, with all the absurd qualities of the models she was following,which have never been better depicted.

If I may be permitted to go back for a moment, I should like to keep the promise I made to take a cursory look at Spain.

To be sure, if knighthood had served as a source of inspiration for our novelists, to what extent had it not also influenced writers on the other side of the Pyrenees? The contents of Don Quixote's library, amusingly catalogued by Miguel Cervantes, clearly demonstrate it; but, however that may be, the renowned author of the memoirs of the greatest madman that any novelist has ever conceived most certainly has no rival worthy of the name. His immortal work, known throughout the world, translated into every language, and perforce considered the foremost novel ever written, doubtless possesses, more than any other novel, the art of storytelling, of blending agreeably the various adventures, and especially of being edifying and amusing. "This book," said Saint-Evremond, "is the only one I reread without getting bored, and the only book I should like to have written." The twelve stories by the same author, highly interesting and full of wit and refinement, definitely place this renowned Spanish novelist in the front rank; without him we might possibly not have had either Scarron's charming work or the greatest part of Lesage's.

After d'Urfé and his imitators, after the Ariadnes and the Cleopatras, the Pharamonds and the Polixandres—all those works, in short, wherein the hero, after languishing throughout nine volumes, was happy indeed to marry in the tenth—after, I say, all this hodgepodge unintelligible today, there appeared Madame de La Fayette who, albeit beguiled by the languorous tone she found in the works of her predecessors, none the less shortened them considerably. And in becoming more concise she became more interesting. It has been said that, because she was a woman (as though this sex, natually more delicate, more given to writing novels, could not aspire in the realm of fiction to many more laurels than we), it has been claimed, I say, that Madame de La Fayette was aided a great deal, and was able to write her novels only with the help of La Rochefoucauld with what regards the reflections and of de Segrais with what regards the style; be that as it may, there is nothing more interesting than *Zayde,* nor any work more agreeably written than *La Princesse de Clèves.* Gracious and charming lady, though the graces may have held your brush, is love not sometimes allowed to guide it?

Fénelon appeared on the scene and thought to make his mark by poetically offering guidance to sovereigns who never paid him any heed. Voluptuous lover of Guyon, your soul had need to love, your mind felt the need to paint; if only you had forsaken pedantry or your pride in teaching kings how one ought to rule, we would have had from your pen more than one masterpiece, rather than a single book which no one reads any longer. The same cannot be said for you, delightful Scarron, till the end of time, your immortal novel will provoke laughter, your scenes will never grow old or outdated. Télemachus, who had but one century to live, will perish beneath the ruins of this century which already is no more; and your actors from Le Mans, gracious and beloved child of madness, will amuse even the most serious readers, so long as men shall dwell upon the face of the earth.

Toward the end of the same century, the daughter of the celebrated Poisson (Madame de Gomez), penned works in a manner far different from the writers of her own sex who had preceded her, but they were no less pleasant; and her *Journées amusantes,* as well as her *Cents nouvelles,* will, despite their shortcomings, always form the nucleus of the library for those who enjoy this kind of writing. Gomez understood her art, 'twould be impossible to refuse her this rightful encomium. Mademoiselle de Lussan, Mesdames de Tencin and de Graffigny, Elie de Beaumont, and Riccoboni vied with her; their writings, full of refinement and taste, are most assuredly an honor to their sex. De Graffigny's *Lettres d'une Péruvienne* will always remain a model of tenderness and sentiment, and those of Mylady Catesby, by Riccoboni, could serve eternally as a model to those who aspire to naught but grace and lightness of touch.

But let us return to the century we left, urged on by the desire to render homage to the gracious women who held sway in this kind of writing, wherefrom the men could learn most excellent lessons.

The Epicureanism of writers such as Ninon de Lenclos, Marion Delorme, the Marquise de Sévigné and the Messieurs La Fare, de Chaulieu, de Saint-Evremond—in short of all that charming group which, awakening from the languors of the goddess of Cytherea, began to come around to Buffon's opinion "that there is naught that is good in love save the physical"—soon changed the tone of the novel.

The writers who emerged thereafter sensed that earlier insipidities would no longer amuse a century perverted by the Regency, a century which had recovered from the follies of chivalry, the absurdities of religion, and the adoration of women, and which, finding it simpler to amuse or to corrupt these women than to serve them or shower fulsome praise upon them, created scenes, situations, and conversations more in keeping with the spirit of the times: they clothed cynicism and immorality in a pleasant, bantering, and sometimes even philosphical style, and at least gave pleasure if they did not edify.

Crébillon wrote *Le Sopha, Tanzaï, Les Egarements de coeur et d'esprit,* etc.—all novels which indulged vice and strayed from virtue but which, when they were offered to the public, were greeted with great success.

Marivaux, more original in his manner of portraying, and terser in style, at least offered convincing characters, captivated the heart and made his public weep. But how, with all that energy, could anyone possess a style so precious and mannered? He is proof positive that Nature never accords the novelist all the gifts required to perfect his art.

Voltaire's goal was quite different: having no other purpose in mind than to insert philosophy into his novels, he gave up everything else in exchange. And with what skill he succeeded in attaining his goal! And, despite all the criticism, *Candide* and *Zadig* will always remain pure masterpieces!

Rousseau, to whom Nature had granted in refinement and sentiment what she had granted only in wit to Voltaire, treated the novel in another way altogether. What vigor, what energy in *La Nouvelle Héloïse*! While Momus was dictating *Candide* to Voltaire, love was etching with its flaming torch every burning page of *Julie,* and we can safely assert that this sublime book will never be bettered; may that truth cause the pen to fall from the hands of that legion of ephemeral writers who, for the past thirty years, have continued to pour out poor imitations of that immortal original; let them be made to feel that, in order to equal that work, they would have to possess a fiery soul like Rousseau's and a philosophic mind such as his—two traits Nature does not bring together in a single person more than once a century.

Athwart all that, Marmontel offered us what he called *Moral Tales,* not because he was teaching morality (as one esteemed man of letters has said), but because the tales portrayed our customs, albeit a trifle too much in the mannered style of Marivaux. What, in fact, do these tales add up to? Puerilities, written solely for women and children, and indeed 'twould be hard to conceive that they came from the same hand as *Bélisaire,* a work which in itself would be enough to assure the author's fame; did he who had written the fifteenth chapter of this book have to aspire to the petty fame of having given us these rosy-hued tales?

Finally, the English novels, the vigorous works of Richardson and Fielding, arrived to teach the French that 'tis not by portraying the fastidious languors of love or the tedious conversations of the bedchamber that one can obtain any success with the novel, but by depicting robust and manly characters who, playthings and victims of that effervescence of the heart known as love, reveal to us both its dangers and its misfortunes; only by so doing can this evolution be shown, this portrayal of passions so carefully traced in the English novels. 'Tis Richardson, 'tis Fielding, who have taught us that the profound study of man's heart—Nature's veritable labyrinth—alone can inspire the novelist, whose work must make us see man not only as he is, or as he purports to be—which is the duty of the historian—but as he is capable of being when subjected to the modifying influences of vice and the full impact of passion. Therefore we must know them all, we must employ every passion and vice, if we wish to labor in this field. From these works we also learn that 'tis not always by making virtue triumph that a writer arouses interest; that we most certainly ought to tend in that direction, insofar as it is possible, but that this rule, which exists neither in Nature nor in the works of Aristotle, is simply one that we should like all men to follow for our own sake and happiness, and is in no wise essential in the novel, nor is't even the one most likely to awaken the reader's interest. For when virtue triumphs, the world is in joint and things as they ought to be, our tears are stopped even, as it were, before they begin to flow. But if, after severe trials and tribulations, we finally witness virtue overwhelmed by vice, our hearts are inevitably rent assunder, and the work having moved us deeply, having, as Diderot was wont to say, "smitten our hearts in reverse," must inevitably arouse that interest which alone can assure the writer of his laurels.

Imagine for a moment: if the immortal Richardson, after twelve or fifteen volumes, had *virtuously* concluded by converting Lovelace, and by having him *peacefully* marry Clarissa, would the reader, when the novel was thus turned round, have shed the delightful tears it now wrings from every sensitive soul?

'Tis therefore Nature that must be seized when one labors in the field of fiction, 'tis the heart of man, the most remarkable of her works, and in no wise virtue, because virtue, however becoming, however necessary it may be, is yet but one of the many facets of this amazing heart, whereof the profound study is so necessary to the novelist, and the novel, the faithful mirror of this heart, must perforce explore its every fold.

Learned translator of Richardson, Prévost, you to whom we are indebted for having rendered into our language the beauties of that renowned author, do you yourself not also deserve an equal share of praise for your own work? And is't not only fair and right that you are called the *French Richardson*? You alone had the ability to hold the reader's attention for a long period by complex and intricate fables, by always sustaining one's interest though dividing it; you alone were sparing enough of your episodes that interest in your main plot waxed rather than waned as they grew more numerous and more complex. Thus that multitude of events wherewith Laharpe reproaches you is not only the source in your work of the most sublime effects, 'tis also what proves most clearly both the quality of your mind and the excellence of your talent. Finally (to add to our own opinion of Prévost what others have thought as well), "*Les Mémoires d'un homme de qualité, Cleveland, L'Histoire d'une Grecque moderne, Le Monde moral,* and above all *Manon Lescaut*[6] are filled with touching and terrible scenes which invincibly affect and involve the reader. The situations in these works, so beautifully arranged, derive from those moments when Nature shudders with horror," etc. And this, then, is what is called writing a novel; these are the qualities which will assure Prévost a posterity his rivals can never hope to attain.

Thereafter follow the writers of the middle of the present century: Dorat, as mannered as Marivaux, as cold and amoral as Crébillon, but a more pleasing writer than either of the two with whom we have compared him: the frivolity of his century excuses his own, and he had the ability to depict it vividly.

Will the charming author of the *Reine de Golconde* allow me to offer him a toast to his talent? We have rarely encountered a more agreeable wit, and the loveliest tales of the century are not the equal of the tale whereby you gained immortality; at once more charming and more felicitous than Ovid, since the Hero-Saviour of France proves, by recalling you to the bosom of your country, that he is as much the friend of Apollo as of Mars: respond to the hope of this great man by adding yet a few more roses to fair Aline's breast.

D'Arnaud, a disciple of Prévost, can often claim to surpass him; both dip their pens into the waters of the Styx, but d'Arnaud oft tempers his upon the flanks of Elysium. Prévost, more vigorous, never altered the tones wherewith he painted *Cleveland*.

R***[7] floods the public with his works; he needs a printing press at the head of his bed. Fortunately, one press alone will groan beneath the weight of his *terrible output;* his is a vile, pedestrian style, his adventures are disgusting, inevitably taken from the lowest, meanest milieux; a gift of prolixity his sole merit, for which only the pepper merchants are grateful to him.

Perhaps at this point we ought to analyze these new novels in which sorcery and phantasmagoria constitute practically the entire merit: foremost among them I would place *The Monk,* which is superior in all respects to the strange flights of Mrs. Radcliffe's brilliant imagination. But that would take us too far afield. Let us concur that this kind of fiction, whatever one may think of it, is assuredly not without merit: 'twas the inevitable result of the revolutionary shocks which all of Europe has suffered. For anyone familiar with the full range of misfortunes wherewith evildoers can beset mankind, the novel became as difficult to write as monotonous to read. There was not a man alive who had not experienced in the short span of four or five years more misfortunes than the most celebrated novelist could portray in a century. Thus, to compose works of interest, one had to call upon the aid of hell itself, and to find in the world of make-believe things wherewith one was fully familiar merely by delving into man's daily life in this age of iron. Ah! but how many disadvantages there are in this manner of writing! The author of *The Monk* has avoided them no more than has Mrs. Radcliffe. Here, there are perforce two possibilities: either one resorts increasingly to wizardry—in which case the reader's interest soon flags—or one maintains a veil of secrecy, which leads to a frightful lack of verisimilitude. Should this school of fiction produce a work excellent enough to attain its goal without foundering upon one or the other of these two reefs, then we, far from denigrating its methods, will be pleased to offer it as a model.

Before broaching our third and final question ("What are

the rules one must follow in order to succeed in prefecting the art of the novel?"), we must, it would seem to me, reply to the constant objection of certain melancholy minds who, to give themselves a gloss of morality wherefrom their hearts are often far distant, persist in asking: "Of what use are novels?"

Of what use, indeed! hypocritical and perverse men, for you alone ask this ridiculous question; they are useful in portraying you as you are, proud creatures who wish to elude the painter's brush, since you fear the results, for the novel is—if 'tis possible to express oneself thuswise—the representation of secular customs, and is therefore, for the philosopher who wishes to understand man, as essential as is the knowledge of history. For the etching needle of history only depicts man when he reveals himself publicly, and then 'tis no longer he: ambition, pride cover his brow with a mask which portrays for us naught but these two passions, and not the man. The novelist's brush, on the contrary, portrays him from within. . .seizes him when he drops this mask, and the description, which is far more interesting, is at the same time more faithful. This, then, is the usefulness of novels, O you cold censors who dislike the novel: you are like that legless cripple who was wont to say: and why do artists bother to paint full-length portraits?

If 'tis therefore true that the novel is useful, let us not fear to outline here a few principles which we believe necessary to bring this kind of literature to perfection. I realize full well that it is difficult to accomplish this task without supplying my enemies with ammunition they can use against me. Shall I not become doubly guilty of not *writing well* if I prove that I know how one must proceed in order to *write well*? Ah! let us put these vain conjectures aside, let us offer them up as sacrifices to the love of art.

The most essential requirement for the novelist's art is most certainly a knowledge of the human heart. Now, every man of intelligence will doubtless second us when we assert that this important knowledge can only be acquired through an intimate acquaintance with *misfortune* and through *travel*. One must have seen men of all nations in order to know them well, and one must have suffered at their hands in order to learn how to judge and evaluate them; the hand of misfortune, by ennobling the character of him whom she crushes, places him at that proper perspective from which it is essential to study men; from this perspective, he views them as a traveler perceives the wild waves crashing against the reefs whereon the tempest has tossed him. But no matter what the situation wherein Nature or destiny has placed him, let the novelist, would he know the hearts of men, be sparing of his own conversation when he is with them. One learns nothing when one speaks; one only learns by listening. And that is why the garrulous and the gossips are generally fools.

O you who wish to venture upon this difficult and thorny career, bear ever in mind that the novelist is the child of Nature, that she has created him to be her painter; if he does not become his mother's lover the moment she gives birth to him, let him never write, for we shall never read him. But if he feels that burning need to portray everything, if, with fear and trembling he probes into the bosom of Nature, in search of his art and for models to discover, if he possesses the fever of talent and the enthusiasm of genius, let him follow the hand that leads him; once having divined man, he will paint him. If his imagination is held in check, let him yield to it, let him embellish what he sees: the fool culls a rose and plucks its petals; the man of genius smells its sweet perfume, and describes it. This is the man we shall read.

But in counseling you to embellish, I forbid you to stray from verisimilitude: the reader has a right to become incensed when he observes that the author is asking too much of him. He can see that he is being deceived, his pride is hurt, he no longer believes anything he reads the moment he suspects he is being misled.

What is more, let no barrier restrain you; exercise at will your right to attack or take liberties with any and all of history's anecdotes, whenever the rupture of this restriction demands it in the formation of the pleasures you are preparing for us. Once again, we do not ask that you be true, but only that you be convincing and credible. To be too demanding of you would be harmful to the pleasure we expect from you. None the less, do not replace the true by the impossible, and let what you invent be well said; you shall be forgiven for substituting your imagination for the truth only when this is done for the express purpose of adorning or impressing; one can never be forgiven for expressing oneself poorly when one has complete freedom of expression. If, like R***, you write *only what everyone already knows,* were you, like him, to give us four volumes a month, better not to put pen to paper at all. No one obliges you to exercise this as your profession; but if you undertake it, do it well. Above all do no choose it merely as a crutch to your existence; your work will reflect your needs, you will transmit your weakness into it; it will have the pallor of hunger: other professions will offer themselves to you: make shoes, but refrain from writing books. We shall not think any the less of you, and since you will not be a source of annoyance to us, we may even like you all the more.

Once you have your outline down on paper, work zealously to enlarge and improve upon it, without however respecting the limitations it seems initially to impose upon you: were you to adhere strictly to this method, your work would be cold and lack breadth. We want outbursts from you, flights of fancy rather than rules. Transcend your drafts, vary them, elaborate upon them: work is the surest source of inspiration. What makes you believe that the inspiration you receive while working is any poorer than that dictated by your outline? Basically, all I ask of you is this one thing: to sustain interest throughout, to the very last page. You shall miss the mark if you punctuate your tale by incidents either repeated too often or which stray too far afield from the main subject. Let those you do make so bold as to indulge in be as well polished as the main plot. You must make amends to the reader when you oblige him to leave something which interests him in order to begin a secondary plot. He may allow you to interrupt him, but he will not forgive you if you bore him or tax his patience. Therefore let your side plots derive from and return to the main plot. If you make your heroes travel, be familiar with the country whereto you take them, carry your magic to the point of identifying me with them; remember that I am walking close beside them in every region to which you take them. Remember too that I may be better informed than you; I shall not forgive a lack of verisimilitude with what regards customs or a slip with what regards dress, and even less an error in geography: as no one compels you to embark upon these escapades, 'tis essential that your local color be exact, else you must remain back home by your fireside. 'Tis the only case in your work when we will not tolerate the make-believe, unless the country you take me to be imaginary; and even in that case, I shall always demand verisimilitude.

Avoid the affectation of moralizing: it has no place in a novel. If the characters your plot requires are sometimes obliged to reason, let them always do so without affectation, without the pretension of doing so. 'Tis never the author who should moralize but the character, and even then you should only allow him to do so when forced by the circumstances.

When you arrive at the denouement, let it occur naturally, let it never be stiff or contrived, but always born of the circumstances. I do not require of you, as do the authors of the *Encyclopédie,* that the denouement be in accordance with the wishes of the reader: what pleasure is there left to him when he has divined everything? The denouement must be the logical result of a threefold demand: the events that lead up to it, the requirements of verisimilitude, and the imagination's inspiration. And if, then, with these principles wherewith I charge your mind, and with your tendency to elaborate, you do not write well, you will at least perform better than we.

For we must confess, in the stories that you are about to read, the audacious effort we have been so bold as to make does not always adhere strictly to the rules of the art. But we trust that extreme verisimilitude of the characters will perhaps compensate for it. Nature, even stranger than the moralists portray it to us, continually eludes the restricting limitations which their policy would like to impose. Uniform in her framework, unpredictable in her effects, Nature's constantly troubled bosom resembles the depths of a volcano, whence there rumble forth in turn either precious stones serving man's needs or fire balls which annihilate them; mighty when she peoples the earth with such as Antonius and Titus; frightful when she spews forth an Andronicus or a Nero; but always sublime, always majestic, always worthy of our studies, of our brush strokes, and of our respectful admiration, because her designs are unknown to us, because 'tis never upon what those designs cause us to feel that we, slaves to her whims or needs, should base our feelings toward her, but upon her grandeur, her energy, no matter what the results may be.

As minds grow increasingly corrupt, as a nation grows older, by virtue of the fact that Nature is increasingly studied and better analyzed, in order for prejudice to be increasingly eradicated, all these things must be made more widely known. This holds equally true for all the arts; 'tis only by advancing that any art moves nearer to perfection; the goal can only be reached by successive attempts. Doubtless we could not have advanced so far in those trying times of ignorance when, weighed down beneath the yoke of religion, whosoever valued the arts risked the penalty of death for his efforts; when talent had as its reward the stakes of the Inquisition. But in the state wherein we live today, let us always start from this principle: when man has weighed and considered all his restrictions, when, with a proud look his eyes gauge his barriers, when, like the Titans, he dares to raise his bold hand to heaven and, armed with his passions, as the Titans were armed with the lavas of Vesuvius, he no longer fears to declare war against those who in times past were a source of fear and trembling to him, when his *aberrations* now seem to him naught but errors rendered legitimate by his studies —should we then not speak to him with the same fervor as he employs in his own behavior? In a word, is eighteenth-century man therefore identical with the man of the eleventh century?

Let us conclude with a positive reassurance that the stories we are presenting today are absolutely new and in no wise a mere reworking of already oft-told tales. This quality is perhaps not without some merit in an age when everything seems already to have been written, when the sterile imaginations of authors seem incapable of producing anything new, and when the public is offered naught save compilations, extracts, and translations.

Still, we should mention that *La Tour enchantée* and *La Conspiration d'Amboise* have some basis in historical fact. We mention this to show the reader, by our candor, how far we are from wishing to deceive him on this score. In this type of fiction, one must be original or refrain from indulging in it.

Regarding the one and the other of these two stories, here is what the reader will find in the sources indicated below.

The Arab historian Abul Kasim Terif ibn-Tariq, whose work is little known amongst our men of letters today, relates the following in connection with *La Tour enchantée:* "Out of sensual pleasure, the effeminate prince Rodrigue enticed to his court his vassals' daughters, and abused them. Amongst them was Florinde, the daughter of Count Julian. Rodrigue violated the girl. The girl's father, who was in Africa, learned of the news from a letter, couched in the form of an allegory, sent him by his daughter. He roused the Moors to revolt and returned to Spain at the head of a Moorish army. Rodrigue is at a loss what to do: his treasury is empty. Hearing there is an immense fortune buried in the Enchanted Tower near Toledo, Rodrigue goes there. He enters the tower, and there sees a statue of Time, which strikes with its staff and, by means of an inscription, enumerates to Rodrigue the list of misfortunes which await him. The prince advances and sees a large tank of water, but no money. He retraces his steps and orders the tower to be sealed. The edifice vanishes in a clap of thunder, and not a trace of it remains. In spite of the dire predictions, Rodrigue amasses an army, wages war for eight days hard by Cordova, and is killed. No trace of his body was every found."

So much for the historical facts. If one will now read our work, he will see whether or not the multitude of events wherewith we have surrounded this dry historical event merits our considering the anecdote as properly our own invention.[8]

As for *La Conspiration d'Amboise,* let the reader consult Garnier and he will see how little indebted we are to history in this story.

No guide has broken ground for us in the other stories: plot, style, episodes—all are our own invention. It may be said that these are not what is best in our work. No matter; we have always believed, and we shall continue to believe, that 'tis better to invent, albeit poorly than to translate or copy. The inventor can lay claim to talent or genius, and has at least that much in his favor; what claim can the plagiarist make? I know of no baser profession, nor do I conceive of any avowal more humiliating than that which such men are obliged to make to themselves, namely, that they are totally lacking in wit, since they are obliged to borrow the wit of others.

Regarding the translator, God forbid that we fail to give him his due. But all he does is add to the luster of our rivals; and if only for the honor of the Nation, were it not best to say to these proud rivals: *and we too know how to create.*

Finally, I must reply to the reproach leveled at me when *Aline et Valcour* was published. My brush, 'twas said, was too vivid. I depict vice with too hateful a countenance. Would anyone care to know why? I have no wish to make vice seem attractive. Unlike Crébillon and Dorat, I have not set myself the dangerous goal of enticing women to love characters who deceive them; on the contrary, I want them to loathe these characters. 'Tis the only way whereby one can avoid being duped by them. And, in order to succeed in that purpose, I painted that hero who treads the path of vice with features so frightful that they will most assuredly not inspire either pity or love. In so doing, I dare say, I am become more moral than those who believe they have license to embellish them. The pernicious works by these authors are like those fruits from America beneath whose highly polished skins there lurk the seeds of death. This betrayal of Nature, the motive of which 'tis not incumbent upon us to reveal, is not done for man. Never, I say it again, never shall I portray crime other than clothed in the colors of hell. I wish people to see crime laid bare, I want them to fear it and detest it, and I know no other way to achieve this end than to paint it in all its horror. Woe unto those who surround it with roses! their views are far less pure, and I shall never emulate them. Given which, let no one any longer ascribe to me the authorship of *J. . . . . .;*[9] I have never written any such works, and I surely never shall. They are naught but imbeciles or evildoers who, despite the authenticity of my denials, can still suspect me of being the author of that work, and I shall henceforth use as my sole arm against their calumnies the most sovereign contempt.

NOTES

[1]The English term "novel" derives from the French *nouvelle* (short story) and the Latin *nouvellus,* the diminutive of *novus* (new). But Sade, in his etymological and historical ruminations, is referring of course to the French equivalent, that is to the term *roman.* It might have made more sense, in translating, to use the English "romance," a cognate of the word around which Sade theorizes. But in English this word has become too colored, and limited to a certain type of frivolous fiction. Throughout this essay, therefore, for Sade's *roman* the term "novel" has been used.—*Tr.*

[2]Actually, the various Romance languages retain in general only a few words and expressions from the language native to each region prior to the advent of the Latin. In French, less than a hundred words can be traced back to the Celtic.—*Tr.*

[3]That is, the Merovingian and the Carolingian.—*Tr.*

[4]*Hercule* is a generic name, made up of two Celtic words, *Her-Coule,* which means Sir-Captain. *Hercoule* was the name given to a general in the army, and thus there were a goodly number of *Hercoules.* Mythology subsequently attributed the amazing feats of several to one. (See *Histoire des Celtes,* by Peloutier.)

[5]Founder, in 978 A.D., of the Capetian dynasty, the third dynasty of French kings which ruled, through fourteen kings in direct succession, until 1328.—*Tr.*

[6]What tears one sheds upon reading this delightful work! How beautifully is Nature portrayed therein, and how interest is not only sustained but successively heightened! How many difficulties are overcome! Think of all the philosophers it would take to provoke that interest in a ruined girl. Would it be too much of an exaggeration to dare suggest that this work deserves the title of our finest novel? 'Twas therein Rousseau saw that, despite imprudences and oversights, a heroine could still manage to touch our hearts; and perhaps we would never have had *Julie* without *Manon*

Lescaut.

[7]Sade here refers to Restif de la Bretonne, whom he loathed personally as much as he loathed his works.—*Tr.*

[8]This anecdote is the one which opens the Brigandas episode in that section of the novel *Aline et Valcour* which bears the title: *Sainville et Léonore,* and interrupts the episode of the body discovered in the tower. Those who have plagiarized this episode word for word have likewise not neglected to copy verbatim the first four lines of this anecdote, which is spoken by the chief of the Bohemians. It is therefore essential for us here to point out to those who buy novels that the works currently on sale at Pigoreau and Leroux's bookshop under the title *Valmor et Lidia,* and at Clérioux and Moutardier's under the title *Alzonde et Koradin,* are absolutely one and the same, and both have been plagiarized verbatim from the *Sainville et Léonore* episode, which forms approximately three volumes of my work entitled *Aline et Valcour.*

[9]Sade is, of course, alluding to *Justine.*—*Tr.*

SELECTED BIBLIOGRAPHY

Billy, André. *L'abbé Prévost.* Paris: Flammarion, 1969.

Bourgeacq, Jacques. *Art et technique de Marivaux dans le Paysan parvenu.* Monte Carlo, Monaco: Regain, 1975.

Brady, Patrick. "Structural Affiliations of *La Nouvelle Héloïse.*" *Esprit créateur,* vol. I, no. 4 (Fall, 1969), 207-18.

Brooks, Peter. *The Novel of Worldliness: Crébillon, Marivaux, Laclos.* Princeton, N. J.: Princeton University Press, 1969.

Carr, J. L. "The secret chain of the *Lettres persanes.*" *Studies on Voltaire and the Eighteenth Century,* 55 (1967), 333-44.

Catrysse, Jean. *Diderot et la mystification.* Paris: Nizet, 1970.

Chauvigny, Louis de. *Lettres inédites de Choderlos de Laclos.* Paris: Société du Mercure de France, 1904.

Cherpack, Clifton. *An Essay on Crébillon fils.* Durham, N. C.: Duke University Press, 1962.

Chouillet, Jacques. *La Formation des idées esthétiques de Diderot: 1745-1763.* Paris: Colin, 1973.

Conroy, Peter. *Crébillon fils: Techniques of the Novel.* (*Studies on Voltaire and the Eighteenth Century,* 99). Banbury, Oxfordshire: Thorpe Mandeville House, 1972.

Coulet, Henri. *Le roman jusqu'à la Révolution.* Paris: Colin, 1967.

Dédéyan, Charles. *Jean-Jacques Rousseau et la sensibilité littéraire à la fin du XVIIIe siècle.* Paris: Société d'édition d'enseignement supérieur, 1966.

Deloffre, Frédéric. *Préciosité nouvelle: Marivaux et le marivaudage*. Paris: Colin, 1967.

—. "Premières Idées de Marivaux sur l'art du roman." *Esprit créateur*, Vol. I, no. 4 (Winter, 1961), 178-83.

Dieckmann, Henri. *Cinq Leçons sur Diderot*. Geneva: Droz, 1959.

—. "The Préface-Annexe of *La Religieuse*." *Diderot Studies*, 2 (1952), 21-147.

Ebel, Miriam. "Crébillon fils, moraliste." Ph.D. dissertation, University of Iowa, 1973.

Elissa-Rhais, Roland. "Une Influence anglaise dans *Manon Lescaut*." *Revue de littérature comparée*, 7 (1927), 619-49.

Ellrich, Robert. "The Structure of Diderot's *Bijoux indiscrets*." *Romanic Review*, 52 (1961), 279-89.

Forno, Lawrence J. "Robert Challe and the Eighteenth Century." *Studies on Voltaire and the Eighteenth Century*, 79 (1971), 163-75.

Forster, E. M. *Aspects of the Novel*. New York: Harcourt-Brace, 1927.

Frautschi, Richard. "La Chaîne secrète des *Lettres persanes*." *French Review*, 44 (1967), 604-12.

Fusil, C.-A. *L'Anti-Rousseau, ou Les Egarements du coeur et de l'esprit*. Paris: Plon, 1929.

Gazagne, Emile. *Marivaux par lui-même*. Paris: Seuil, 1958.

Green, Frederick C. *Minuet: Literary Ideas in Eighteenth-Century France and England*. New York: Ungar, 1966.

Grimsley, Ronald. "L'Ambiguité dans l'oeuvre de Diderot." *Cahiers de l'Association internationale des études françaises*, 13 (1961), 223-38.

Guéhenno, Jean. *Jean-Jacques: Roman et vérité*. Paris: Grasset, 1950.

Guyon, Bernard. "Notes sur l'art du roman dans *Manon Lescaut*." Pp. 185-92 of *Hommage au Doyen Etienne Gros*. Gap: Louis-Jean, 1959.

Jaccard, Jean-Luc. *Manon Lescaut: le personnage romancier.* Paris: Nizet, 1975.

Jones, Silas P. *A List of French Prose Fiction from 1700 to 1750.* New York: Wilson, 1939.

Kempf, Roger. *Diderot et le roman.* Paris: Seuil, 1964.

Kra, Pauline. "The Invisible Chain of the *Lettres persanes.*" *Studies on Voltaire and the Eighteenth Century,* 23 (1963), 9-60.

Lanson, Gustave. *Histoire de la littérature française.* Paris: Hachette, 1906.

Laufer, Roger. *Lesage, ou le métier de romancier.* Paris: Gallimard, n.d.

—. "La réussite romanesque et la signification des *Lettres Persanes.*" *Revue de l'histoire littéraire,* 61 (1961), 188-203.

—. "Structure et signification de *Jacques le fataliste.*" *Revue des sciences humaines,* 112 (1963), 517-35.

—. *Style rococo, style des lumières.* Paris: Corti, 1963.

Lecercle, Jean-Louis. "Inconscient et création littéraire: sur la *Nouvelle Héloïse.*" *Etudes littéraires,* I (1968), 197-204.

—. *Rousseau et l'art du roman.* Paris: Colin, 1969.

Lemieux, Raymond. "Le Jeu des temps comme moyen d'action et d'analyse dans les *Liaisons dangereuses.*" Ph.D. dissertation, University of Iowa, 1969.

Loy, J. R. *Diderot's Determined Fatalist.* New York: Kings Crown Press, 1950.

—. *Montesquieu.* New York: Twayne, 1968.

Lynch, Lawrence W. "The Critical Preface to *Les Egarements du coeur et de l'esprit.*" *French Review,* Vol. 51, no. 5 (April, 1978), 657-65.

—. "Richardson's Influence on the Concept of the Novel in Eighteenth-Century France." *Comparative Literature Studies,* Vol. 14, no. 3 (September, 1977), 233-43.

Mahmoud, Parvine. "Les Persans de Montesquieu." *French Review*, 34 (1960), 44-50.

Marmontel, Jean-François. *Eléments de littérature*. 3 vols. Paris: Didot, 1867.

Mauzi, Robert. "La Parodie romanesque dans *Jacques le fataliste*." *Diderot Studies*, 6 (1964), 89-132.

May, Georges. *Diderot et la Religieuse*. New Haven, Conn.: Yale University Press, 1964.

—. *Le Dilemme du roman au XVIIIe siècle*. Paris: Presses universitaires, 1963.

—. "L'Histoire a-t-elle engendré le roman?" *Revue de l'histoire littéraire*, 55 (1955), 155-76.

—. *Rousseau par lui-même*. Paris: Seuil, 1961.

Mead, William. "*Les Liaisons dangereuses* and Moral Usefulness." *PMLA*, 75 (1960), 563-70.

Mercier, Roger. "Le Roman dans les *Lettres persanes:* structure et signification." *Revue des sciences humaines*, 108 (1962), 345-56.

Monty, Jeanne. *Les Romans de l'abbé Prévost*. (*Studies on Voltaire and the Eighteenth Century*, 78). Banbury, Oxfordshire: Thorpe Mandeville House, 1970.

Mornet, Daniel. *Introduction à la Nouvelle Héloïse*. Paris: Hachette, 1925.

—. *La Nouvelle Héloïse de Jean-Jacques Rousseau*. Paris: Mellottée, 1928.

—. *La Pensée française au XVIIIe siècle*. Paris: Colin, 1965.

—. *Rousseau*. Paris: Hatier, 1950.

Mylne, Vivienne. *The Eighteenth-century French Novel: Techniques of Illusion*. New York: Barnes and Nobel, 1965.

Nardin, Pierre. "La Recette stylistique des *Lettres persanes*." *Français moderne,* 20 (1952), 277-86.

O'Reilly, Robert. "The Structure and Meaning of the *Lettres persanes.*" *Studies on Voltaire and the Eighteenth Century,* 67 (1969), 91-131.

Osmont, Robert. "Remarques sur la genèse et la composition de la *Nouvelle Héloïse.*" *Annales Jean-Jacques Rousseau,* 33 (1953-55), 93-148.

Palmer, Benjamin. "Crébillon fils and His Reader." *Studies on Voltaire and the Eighteenth Cenury,* 132 (1975), 183-97.

Pizzorusso, Arnaldo. *La Poetica del romanzo in Francia, 1660-1685.* Rome: Salvatore Sciascia, 1962.

Ratner, Moses. *Theory and Criticism of the Novel from l'Astrée to 1750.* New York: De Palma, 1938.

Rétat, Pierre, ed. *Les Paradoxes du romancier: Les Egarements de Crébillon fils.* Grenoble: Presses universitaires, 1975.

Romberg, Bertil. *Studies in the Narrative Technique of the First-Person Novel.* Stockholm: Almquist and Wicksell, 1962.

Rosbottom, Ronald. *Marivaux's Novels: Theme and Function in Early Eighteenth-century Narrative.* Rutherford, N. J.: Fairleigh Dickinson University Press, 1974.

Rousset, Jean. *Forme et signification.* Paris: Corti, 1962.

—. "La Monodie épistolaire: Crébillon fils." *Etudes littéraires,* 1 (1968), 167-74.

—. "Prévost romancier: la forme autobiographique." Pp. 197-205 of *Actes du Colloque d'Aix-en-Provence.* Aix: Presses universitaires, 1965.

Seylaz, Jean-Luc. *Les Liaisons dangereuses et la création romanesque chez Laclos.* Geneva: Droz, 1958.

—. "Structure et signification dans *Manon Lescaut.*" *Etudes des lettres,* 4 (1961), 97-108.

Sgard, Jean. *Prévost romancier.* Paris: Corti, 1958.

Shackleton, Robert. *Montesquieu.* Oxford: Oxford University Press, 1961.

Showalter, English. *The Evolution of the French Novel, 1641-1789.* Princeton, N. J.: Princeton University Press, 1972.

Starobinski, Jean. *Montesquieu par lui-même.* Paris: Seuil, 1957.

Stewart, Philip. *Imitation and Illusion in the French Memoir Novel, 1700-1750.* New Haven, Conn.: Yale University Press, 1969.

Sturm, Emile. *Crébillon fils et le libertinage au XVIIIe siècle.* Paris: Nizet, 1970.

Thelander, Dorothy. *Laclos and the Epistolary Novel.* Geneva: Droz, 1963.

Thody, Philip. *Laclos: Les Liaisons dangereuses.* London: Camelot Press, 1970.

Thomas, Ruth P. *"Jacques le fataliste, Les Liaisons dangereuses and the Autonomy of the Novel." Studies on Voltaire and the Eighteenth Century,* 117 (1974), 239-49.

Vailland, Roger. *Laclos par lui-même.* Paris: Seuil, 1959.

Versini, Laurent. *Laclos et la tradition du roman épistolaire.* Paris: Klincksieck, 1968.

Watt, Ian. *The Rise of the Novel: Studies in Defoe, Richardson and Fielding.* Berkeley: University of California Press, 1957.

Wilson, Arthur. *Diderot: The Testing Years.* New York: Oxford University Press, 1957.